Cultural Memory

Cultural Memory
RESISTANCE, FAITH & IDENTITY

Jeanette Rodríguez & Ted Fortier

UNIVERSITY *of* TEXAS PRESS
AUSTIN

Requests for permission to reproduce material
from this work should be sent to:
   Permissions
   University of Texas Press
   P.O. Box 7819
   Austin, TX 78713-7819
   www.utexas.edu/utpress/about/bpermission.html

∞ The paper used in this book meets the minimum requirements
of ANSI/NISO Z39.48–1992 (R1997) (Permanence of Paper).

LIBRARY OF CONGRESS CATALOGING-IN-PUBLICATION DATA

Rodríguez, Jeanette, 1954–
   Cultural memory : resistance, faith, and identity / Jeanette
Rodríguez and Ted Fortier. — 1st ed.
      p.   cm.
   Includes bibliographical references and index.
      ISBN-13: 978-0-292-71663-6 (cloth : alk. paper)
      ISBN-10: 0-292-71663-X (cloth : alk. paper)
      ISBN-13: 978-0-292-71664-3 (pbk. : alk. paper)
      ISBN-10: 0-292-71664-8 (pbk. : alk. paper)
   1. Memory—Religious aspects—Christianity—Case studies.
2. Memory—Religious aspects—Case studies.   3. Memory—Social
aspects—Case studies.   4. Christianity and culture—Case studies.
5. Religion and culture—Case studies. I. Fortier, Ted. II. Title.
   BV4597.565.R63 2007
   306.6—dc22
                                                2006033329

To all the elders whose faith-filled struggles and resistance have ensured that their people might live on and continue to teach us the ways of wisdom and peace

Contents

Preface

THE QUESTION OF EXPERIENCE

T HIS MANUSCRIPT IS A RESULT of a dialogue between an anthropologist and a theologian, specifically, between a cultural anthropologist who has spent many years working with various indigenous groups and a theologian who has accompanied various faith communities in Latin America and is a proponent of liberation theologies. For some time now we have been struggling with the question of how to identify and describe the notion of cultural memory. In particular, we are interested in how cultural memory functions and is transmitted among marginalized communities in a constant struggle for survival. Two experiences are crucial sources for the way we have come to understand the dynamics of memory and narrative. One of us, Jeanette Rodríguez, became interested in cultural memory through her discovery of her Jewish roots. She writes:

> I was a religious studies and philosophy major at a New York college where 80 percent of the students were Jewish. I am a "cradle" Roman Catholic and a New York Latina. My parents and brothers emigrated from Ecuador to the United States in 1952. Given my own bilingual and bicultural background, I cannot remember a time when I did not live in creative, ambiguous, or hostile tension. This particular period, however, was one of intense struggle as I wrestled with the questions of religion and meaning in the twentieth century.
>
> A key to this angst was my exposure to, and understanding of, the Holocaust. I thought that anyone in touch with his or her humanity would be outraged by the massacre of many millions of women, men, and children. Yet many of those around me, and certainly our own American culture, seemed blasé about this catastrophic tragedy. My own affective reaction included youthful indignation and a commitment that this should "never again" happen. At home, I attempted to regain inner peace.

One night while at the dinner table with the other members of my family, my father and I entered into a discussion about why I was so "obsessed" with the Holocaust. I suggested that perhaps I identified with a group that yearned to know their God and maintain their culture. As I became more visibly emotional in the discussion, my mother turned to my father and said, "Sangre llama a sangre" [Blood calls to blood]. It is time to tell her."

My father then began to tell his story. He said his family had Jewish roots. As he spoke movingly of his origins, his discourse seemed cautious. While he spoke, several memories began to make sense to me: how my father would drop us off at church on Sundays and then take off—I had thought it was simply a Latin American thing for a man to do; the yarmulke (a skull cap worn by observant Jews) I had seen in one of his drawers when I was in high school—he had explained that he kept it so that he could attend the prayer services of his employer, who was Jewish; how all of my cousins on my father's side in Latin America wore yarmulkes—I had always thought this very strange during my trips there; his swaying back and forth at prayer when he did come to church with us. Once I was informed of this missing piece in my family history, things made sense, and I experienced peace.

Another experience of the profound nature of cultural memory led to the doctoral work of cultural anthropologist Ted Fortier. In his fieldwork among the Indian people of the Columbia Plateau in the western part of the United States, he observed repeatedly the deep connections the Indian people made to the wisdom and ways of their ancestors. Even though over two hundred years of missionary activities, government policies of acculturation, and the steady incursion of Western ideas had made a great impact on the people, they retained a core identity of being "Indian." The manner in which this was lived out was a combination of ritual activities, the telling of kin-based stories, and a persistent outlook on life that resisted the hegemony of a Eurocentric worldview. An example of these deeply held convictions is evident in the following story, collected on the Coeur d'Alene Reservation:

"I do not like anthropologists. I detest what they do, always trying to drag stuff up out of the past. That stuff is over and gone. It's done. It does not do anyone any good. It was painful then, and we are living now. And things are okay now."

Maria looked away from me, out the window and across the field to the new tribal school. It stands on the hill below the old Sister's building, where Maria and generations of Indian girls had gone to boarding school. Maria tossed her long hair over her shoulder and sighed. Her eyes glistened with the first signs of tears.

"Let me tell you something," she said, touching her eyes and looking back at me.

"Four or five years ago that anthropologist, I forget his name— oh, Doctor, at the University—called and told us to come and get some bones of the ancestors. So, Abe, Clem, and me went down to Moscow.

"Doctor met us in his office and took us downstairs in some old building. It was really cold, and I did not know where we were going. It was cold, I did not know why, but later I did. I did not like it at all.

"When we got to this big room full of shelves and boxes, he took down a box and just handed it to Clem. He just took down this big cardboard box, filled with bones of the ancestors, and handed it to us! There, that is it! Just like that! I couldn't believe it. I was crying. I was so upset. But we took the bones and placed them into a parfleche that we had with us.

"Then Clem said, 'Let's sing.' But I could not, not there, and I was too choked up. Clem said that is okay, we'll go somewhere else. So that guy took us upstairs to another room with some windows and left us alone. I told Clem and Abe that I couldn't sing, not there. It was just too much for me. But Clem said we have to, and that it will be okay. And we sang the songs. Then we came back to DeSmet.

"When we got to DeSmet, we took the ancestors into the church, no, wait, we took them into the chapel of the priest's house, and left them by the altar. A week later we were all ready, and we went by pickup caravan up to the mountain. It was so hard, still, and I cried all the way there. We buried them on the mountain, and sang again."

This brief story illustrates quite well one of the limitations of the Western philosophical tradition of modernism that Coeur d'Alene spirituality easily bridges: social-cultural structures are viewed in dichotomous terms. That is, one is *either* a Christian or not, one is *either* an Indian or not, and so on. What the precontact Coeur d'Alene Indians brought to the missionization process was a premodern philosophy that included an integrative conception of being. It was, and is, completely compatible to the Coeur d'Alene to be both a warrior and a soldier of the Sacred Heart (a man of peace); the Creator-Being is not only a Mideastern deity, but also the Grandfather Spirit. The place of worship is not only the church on the hill, but also the open lakes and woodlands and mountains. For Maria and her relatives, being a Coeur d'Alene Indian is a cultural connection that calls from beyond the grave to the people living today and to those still to be born.

Several important elements in the first story differ from that of the Coeur d'Alene Indians. In the Rodríguez family, cultural memory is a serendipitous discovery of a dormant cultural/religious memory of the past that surfaced in the author's consciousness. Crucial to this understanding of a cultural memory was the instinctive need that rose from her personal journey to reveal the "otherness" hidden in her past. This experience of self-discovery, which revealed the "hidden otherness" of who she is, led her to reimagine her past, her culture, and her heritage not only in a new and unforeseen way, but in a way that validates her own existence. What was a moment of self-possession became an act of self-revelation.

Reflection on a personal experience this powerful has the distinguishing element of provoking thought, raising questions, and providing profound insights. The deeper the abyss of crisis is, the greater becomes one's connection to cultural memory and to past generations. The mediating link between personal memory and the collective memory of one's past may be a word, an image, a person, or some specific, concrete thing that makes this otherness erupt in one's consciousness and demands one's attention. This otherness is cultural memory, our past, making a claim on us or, better stated, claiming us as its own. Once this occurs, reality is seen in a different way, that is, in a way that gives meaning to our lives and validates our existence. In short, this different way of seeing things means that not only do we identify with the otherness of our experience, but we see it as our raison d'être.

On a collective level, the constituent elements described above are absent. Cultural memory at the collective level is simply there waiting to be recovered in our songs, our rituals, our ceremonies, our stories, or through other mediating elements. The difference between the personal and the collective level is this: personally, the individual discovers his or her cultural memory through crisis, and collectively, the individual recovers his or her cultural memory through songs, rituals, ceremonies, and other mediating forms. On the personal level, the otherness of cultural memory is hidden from us. On the collective level, the otherness of cultural memory is simply there.

Fortier's story of the Coeur d'Alene Indians is told from the viewpoint of an individual, Maria, whose antagonistic feelings toward "the university anthropologist" who desecrates the remains (bones) of her ancestors represents her feelings for the white man and his institutions (which serve as instruments of oppression). As the story relates, it was up to Abe, Clem, and Maria to go "recover" the bones of their ancestors. The irreverent treatment of the remains by the no-name anthropologist who puts the bones in a "box" gravely threatened the living history within them, leaving the Indians stunned and insulted. Maria could not greet her ancestors with a song while the remains were still inside the university building, but Clem and Abe convinced her that through the mediating form of a song, they would recover the cultural memory of their ancestors. After this, they went back to DeSmet.

Finally, the mediating element of ritual and ceremony became a communal event. After the remains were taken to the church for proper observance and prayer, the caravan of cars accompanied them to the mountain for burial. The Coeur d'Alene Indian story is one of collective cultural memory.

There are two levels of structure in cultural memory that are analogous to the Marxist analysis of the base (the personal level) and the superstructure (the collective level). Over time the base changes, adapts, and transforms itself, sometimes radically. The ideas, values, and ideologies contained within the superstructure rise above the base and take on a life of their own, that is, they become objectified. For example, a medieval feudal base with a monarchical government of kings, queens, and princes slowly gave way to a national base of presidents, prime ministers, and other types of leaders. Thus, as the base changed, the superstructure also changed. This parallels what happens to the personal and collective levels in cultural memory.

Having said this, however, we must also add an important qualifier. The base may change from epoch to epoch (or, at the personal level, from generation to generation), but change also contains the constancy of past epochs. For example, today we no longer live in an industrialized base; this epoch has been replaced by the information age base. Presidents and prime ministers, carryovers from the industrial base, are becoming more and more obsolete as transnational corporations with no allegiance to any particular country are becoming more powerful than the countries themselves. Heads of corporations are now dictating foreign policy. Even in the United States, the revolving door between government officials and corporate board members who trade places during every new administration never stops. The point here is that even though we live in an information age, the rapid changes cannot render obsolete the superstructure (collective memory) of the feudal base; today, though quite anachronistically, we still have kings, queens, and other ranked nobility. The same is true of cultural memory. Generations today are not the same as those who lived five hundred years ago, but their cultural memory still lives in our collective memory.

Acknowledgments

THIS MANUSCRIPT IS THE RESULT of the contributions, generosity, and insights of many people. First and foremost, the authors thank the communities that allowed us to enter their sacred spaces to both witness and share the significance of their culture. We thank the Mexican American community for offering the icon of Our Lady of Guadalupe, and the Yaqui for their survival, rituals, and invitation to pray. We are grateful to the community of El Salvador and to those committed to the church of the martyrs and the church of the poor for their transmission of this ancient truth. This central option for the poor yields wisdom regarding the revelation of God and the meaning of being human. We thank the Tzeltal communities in Chiapas, Mexico, and the Jesuit mission at Bachajón. Their hospitality, welcome, and strength demonstrated the lived reality of resistance while incorporating the wisdom of the Catholic tradition.

A project like this involves many years of fieldwork and on-site research. Therefore, we wish to thank the following foundations and institutions for their encouragement and financial support: the Lilly Theological Scholars Grant; the Association of Theological Schools; the Louisville Institute for the Study of American Religion; Seattle University for a Faculty Research Grant; the Mellon Foundation at St. Louis University; the Jesuit Mission Fund; and the Graduate School of Theology and Ministry at Seattle University. We thank our departments and the colleagues who were willing to read the manuscript and offer their critique, insights, and editorial competency: Sharon Callahan, Jeanne Berwick, Miriam Greenbaum, Juan Alvarez, and Molly Fumia. We thank our research assistants who were our legs and arms in retrieving material and transcribing hundreds of hours of tape: Katie Watt, Christine Swensen, and Mara Buckley. Special thanks to the Theology and Religious Studies administrative assistant, Lauren St. Pierre, for being this project's anchor; and to Rose Zbiegien, of the Department of International Studies, for her assistance in finalizing the index. Finally, we owe a tremendous debt of gratitude to Nancy Warrington, whose meticulous attention to editorial details has been priceless.

Cultural Memory

Introduction

THE SINGLE MOST IMPORTANT ADAPTATION for the survival of the human species is culture. As we will develop in this book, discrete human cultures have survived a plethora of threats to their existence through their ability to interpret, adapt to, and resist hegemonic cultures that are more "powerful." The very key to a species' survival is its ability to adapt to rapidly changing conditions. The human species has survived, in a number of unique configurations, because of the elasticity of culture, which enables groups to access stored wisdom and ways of coping with diverse patterns of existence. The mystery and the very core of this dynamism of culture rest in memory.

Memory is the capacity to remember, to create and re-create our past. "Cultural memory" is a concept introduced to the archaeological disciplines by Jan Assmann,[1] who defines it as the "outer dimension of human memory,"[2] embracing two different concepts: "memory culture" (*Erinnerungskultur*) and "reference to the past" (*Vergangenheitsbezug*). Memory culture is the process by which a society ensures cultural continuity by preserving, with the help of cultural mnemonics, its collective knowledge from one generation to the next, rendering it possible for later generations to *reconstruct* their cultural identity.[3] When we speak about cultural memory, we are including in this definition two distinct characteristics: (1) the survival of a historically, politically, and socially marginalized group of people, and (2) the role of spirituality as a form of resistance.

The definition of culture flows from an understanding that people develop unique sets of categories, including languages, political organizations, and rituals and ceremonies. Historically marginalized groups have additional categories that reveal the cultural forces that have resisted annihilation from dominant groups by accessing forms of spiritual resistance. These are the issues of people who have historically had to fight for their community and maintain a social construct to exist in the world. For Mexican Americans, the Yaqui, the poor, and the Tzeltal, life is a struggle to find a place—that is, establish their presence in the world today and make known their rights not only to survive but to flourish apart from the dominant cultures—in a globalized world that has marginalized them.

Where do marginalized, threatened cultural groups go to find such a place? And by "place" we mean community, landscape, and spirituality, that is, an identity that comes from caring for others and being cared for by a respectful community; from an attachment to land and all of its processes; and, finally, from the awe and wonder of a communal sense of creative knowing. We contend that their struggle to find such an identity is rooted in religious ideology. Religious ideology manifests a spirituality grounded in experience and is endemic to the continuum of self-preservation and reproduction of human beings. This is why we have focused this study on four discrete manners in which four different cultures illustrate how religious ideology constructs pathways for resistance, infusing ideological faith with the implements for producing ethnic identities. These four manifestations are the image of Our Lady of Guadalupe, the secret rituals among the Yaqui Indians, the narrative in the evolving memory of martyred Archbishop Oscar Romero of El Salvador, and the syncretism among the Tzeltal Indians of Chiapas, Mexico. It is our argument that by examining the emotion-laden schemas of religious faith, we can begin to understand the powerful elements of memories that resist assimilation in the world today.

Anthropologists have found that among the earliest *Homo sapiens sapiens* of over 50,000 years ago, or even with the extinct *Homo sapiens neanderthalensis* of over 100,000 years ago, one of the common elements present in their cultural record is sensitivity for religious experience. Religious experience is defined as a belief in a power or a world that lies beyond ordinary human experience. Archaeological evidence shows that these early cultures were conscious of the fact that the world they perceived was not the only reality. They were aware that there is a power, or a being, that exists beyond the physical world that can be known through ordinary experience. This is most easily seen in the presence of grave goods, burial orientation, cave art, the use of figurines, and so on. These symbolic elements, which indicate a reverence for life, sensitivity to another realm of existence, and awe for the human connection to the creative forces of the universe, are the very subjects that give rise to our question, What is the difference between ordinary experience and religious experience?

The above observation regarding the archaeological evidence concerning death and burial practices provides a window into the continuum of meaning in an ordinary life. All human beings die, and death is simply an ordinary experience of existence. What brings the level of ordinary into religious phenomenology, however, is the *meaning* ascribed to ordinary events. Humans are symbol-bearing, symbol-creating beings that need to provide meaning to virtually every aspect of existence. The evolutionary role of emotion seems to be an important element here. In other words, how do we attach emotion-laden schemas to those life events that continue to bring meaning and remembrance throughout not only our existence, but the existence of those who will follow us? This process of connecting emotion to life events is most evident in ritual activity that is filled with symbolic composition and continually repeated.

Thus, at the site of an ancient burial, we find that elements of a man's, a woman's, or a child's connection to life are placed with them: food, tools, pets, or other items. The body is often oriented on an east-west axis, symbolic of the rising and setting of the sun, the voyage of life and death, and renewal. Burial in the earth, a practice in many ancient cultures, is most often associated with the concept of seeds that die, only to be renewed in the next season. Also associated with these burials is the use of red ochre, which is a symbol of blood and through it, life.

Therefore, the ordinary—the death of an organism—becomes a symbol of the worldview of a particular people. The meaning of one individual's existence is symbolically interpreted as valuable and meaningful for the whole group. What remains are things that cannot be answered by ordinary experience. For example, what happens to the vitality of a human when life ceases? Looking at nature, one can observe the cycles of life, the manner in which a plant brings forth new life each year, only to wither and die at some point. It is the human ability to translate that ordinary experience into a sense of awe, wonder, and respect that gives dynamism to a group of human beings and leads to cultural configurations of meaning that are passed from generation to generation.

One of the functions of religion is to answer essential questions as to how the world came about and how humans are related to it. It seeks to explain our earth-centeredness. Why this? Why that? Religion is an attempt to filter meaning into the most difficult questions. As we seek to give meaning to everything we do, religion validates our existence. It deposits forces into the universe that sustain moral order; this in turn sustains the social order of a people. Religion validates our existence by connecting us with ancestors, with spirits, with a god or gods. Religion mediates the dynamic of being here in the moment while also being part of an ongoing continuum. It firmly reinforces our human ability to ascribe meaning to all experience, such as death, illness, famine, birth, or suffering. Religion heightens our communal experience of life. It brings us together in a community that reinforces the events in our lives. Religious experience interprets the way a community defines the world, and it does so in such a way that establishes its primary values, affects, behaviors, and choices.

The reproduction of cultural survival is, then, both a biological and an ideological construction. Research in collective memory and historical identity recognizes that critical to the retaining of one's cultural identity, and assuming survival, are language, religious practices, and the maintenance of the principles regarding everyday life.[4]

"Sangre llama a sangre" (blood calls to blood) is an expression or metaphor that alludes to blood as the carrier of one's life, which is in turn connected to others. It is the life force that allows one to access the affective, intuitive bond of community that surges up without any rigid or rational trappings. It has its own truth, and this truth is "grasped" and needs no affirmation or validation from outside itself. This truth is expressed in narrative, ritual drama, and ceremonies.

In this book, cultural memory, or blood calling out to blood, and evoking recognition of truth are explored as constitutive elements of memory. We will identify and explain these elements in four distinct cultural groups in the Americas. Within these groups, four different aspects of cultural memory will be examined: image, secrecy, narrative, and synchronicity. Each of these is intended to be seen as an example of one aspect of memory—a memory that (1) liberates from oppression, (2) provides a medium for transmission of that memory; (3) informs the emotions of generations; and (4) unites a people through time for a common cause.

We intend to explore this phenomenon by isolating and analyzing the content, transmission, and sources of empowerment, including how such memories are passed on from generation to generation. The four aspects of cultural memory will be explained through the following: the *Mexican American* community and their devotion to the image of Guadalupe, the *Yaqui* and the role of secrecy and ceremony in maintaining their cultural identity, the evolving cultural memory of *Archbishop Oscar Romero* of San Salvador as it is transmitted through the church of the poor and the martyrs, and the synchronism of Catholic *Tzeltal Maya* in the state of Chiapas, Mexico.

What is the source of a memory powerful enough to carry a people even through attempted genocide? Remembering has been a key to survival for Jews, whose identity has long been bound up with oppression and resistance. The key memory for the Jewish community is told in the story of Exodus, which has been the guiding myth for Jewish identity.

Elie Wiesel once said that the reflective Christian knows that it was not the Jewish people that died in Auschwitz, but Christianity.[5] The Jewish theological question after Auschwitz was not only "Where was God?" but also "Where was humanity?" The Catholic theologian Johann Baptist Metz echoes this when he speaks of *memoria passionis* as the only "universal category of humanity open to us . . . I am not thinking of a memory that only serves to affirm us or to secure our identities—rather the opposite: it calls into question our tightly sealed up identities. It is a 'dangerous' memory . . . it is a remembrance that does not use suffering to make us aggressive, but reflects on others who suffer."[6] The failure of humanity, specifically Christian humanity, is not only transmitted through shared memory, but is a symbol of all that threatens Jewish existence.

Our Lady of Guadalupe as a cultural memory is undoubtedly the most significant spiritual and cultural symbol for Mexican Americans. An earlier study by Jeanette Rodríguez demonstrated how the memory of Guadalupe is carried in the culture of a people, both consciously and unconsciously, until it gradually becomes embedded in their values. For Mexican Americans, Our Lady of Guadalupe represents an affirmation of their worth and a positive valuation of their own culture and tradition, thus becoming an empowering symbol that asserts their communal sense as a people.

Juan Alvarez, a colleague and Nahuatl scholar, says that we Mexican Americans do not think or reflect on the meaning of Our Lady of Guadalupe, in much the same way that we do not think of the blood that runs through our veins. We simply know it is there. Yet, one day, as we experience debilitating crisis, something extraordinary called "thinking" happens, or, in some cases, it may not happen at all. Enrique Dussel once said:

> Those who attempt to think about the where and how of their being without starting from a crisis point will not be able to think. Many perhaps have lived their whole lives without any crisis. Yet crisis is a sine qua non for thinking, and the more radical and abysmal the crisis, the greater the possibility for real thought. Crisis comes from the Greek verb *krinein,* meaning to "to judge," but with the added note of distancing oneself.[7]

The Yaqui represent a culture that has endured five hundred years of conquest, enslavement, and religious and civil persecution, yet continues to be resilient despite those forces that have destroyed so many other indigenous cultures. The Yaqui are bound together through a number of secret societies and rituals that have adapted to but not been subverted by modern culture or Jesuit missionary efforts. The Yaqui provide insight into the mechanisms that allow cultural adaptation to occur while maintaining group identity through strict adherence to family and kin-based ritual obligations. The Yaqui culture is characterized by a pervasive spirituality that appears to be based on what we are terming cultural memory.

The memory surrounding murdered Archbishop Oscar Romero, the martyred archbishop of El Salvador, is still emerging. Although the memory of Romero is grounded in the geopolitical arena and the secular world of the wars of resistance in Central America, one cannot think of Romero without thinking about faith and the Roman Catholic tradition in particular. Increasingly, the memory of Romero elicits thoughts and feelings about resistance and other priests, sisters, and laypeople who were murdered for accompanying the oppressed people. More specifically, the narrative of Romero resurrects the memory of the church of the poor and the martyrs. The Catholic Tzeltal Maya are a significant example of the way contemporary synchronicity is worked out.

These four specific cases have been selected because each presents a significant research agenda in its own right, and each permits research on a unique practice of cultural memory within a highly distinctive geographical, political, or religious group. Our intent is not to undertake a definitive comparative analysis, but rather to explore the ways in which these practices sustain collective beliefs, maintain cultural distinctiveness, and stimulate dignity and defiance in the face of injustice.

Research tools utilized in this project include historical study, participant observation, and structured and unstructured interviews. Our aim in this project is to combine the ethnographic field skills of Fortier, a cultural anthropologist, with the analytical and hermeneutical skills of Rodríguez, a liberation theologian. Thus, this book is both a cultural artifact, depicting real people's lived experiences of faith and identity, and an exegesis of that cultural text, as it were, in that we actively interpret the realms that we have delineated for this foray into cultural memory. For us, as we explain in the following chapters, the crucial elements of reflexive ethnography, historical contextualization, and theological advocacy provide a nexus for the telling of four inspiring stories of survival, resistance, and active negotiation in order to maintain a unique niche in the globalized world today.

1. The Concept of Cultural Memory

To be rooted is perhaps the most important and least recognized need of the human soul.

SIMONE WEIL, *The Need for Roots*

HOW WE REMEMBER past events has a profound impact on what we do and how we will live. While personal memory is the cornerstone supporting collective or social memory, memory cannot be understood apart from social forces. Religious, class, and family affiliations that form in cognitive and affective deliberations help construct the manner in which a memory will be interpreted.

Thus, memory is transmitted by a people in their historical, social, and political context. In any given culture, it is the social group that carries forth, from generation to generation, that which they choose to pass on and, perhaps, that which they are not conscious of passing on. In some cases, memory is a distinctly political phenomenon, and requires analysis—possibly the most important aspect of political understanding.[1] With regard to cultural memory, therefore, we contend that a people carry a memory and that the memory itself is also a carrier. One means by which memory is transmitted is through narrative. Narrative emphasizes the active, self-shaping quality of human thought. Its power resides in its ability to create, form, refashion, and reclaim identity. This characteristic of narrative is useful for our work, because it illuminates the diverse modes of attending to and conveying those stories.

> Narratives have trans-subjective truth value, however fuzzily defined it might be. In sum, we propose that narratives (stories) in the human sciences should be defined provisionally as discourses with a clear sequential order that connects events in a meaningful way for a definite audience, and thus offer insights about the world and/ or people's experiences of it.[2]

Memory, as Lewis and Sandra Hinchman argue, has always been the home of narrative. Both as individuals and as members of various groups, our present existence is powerfully shaped by recollections of the past and anticipations of the future. It is through narrative that a culture organizes and integrates its understanding of reality.[3]

Recent literature in sociology on age cohorts suggests the significance of formative events. The disciplines of psychology, anthropology, and theology understand that one's present existence is shaped irrevocably by recollections of the past and anticipations of the future. It is these memories that give meaning, direction, and shape to ethical choices.[4] Without memory, the living of life would have no coherence at all.

Memory, however, is only one modality of experience. It does not exist in isolation from those other modalities that are oriented to the present and the future. It is also significant to note that the way we remember, what we anticipate, and how we perceive are largely social. Our interest in spiritual narratives is grounded in the connection between the unique, personal consciousness of an individual and how that is both informed by and informs the larger community. As Roland Barthes has observed, "There does not exist, and never has existed, a people without narratives."[5] Hinchman and Hinchman add, "Narratives, then, are what constitute community. They explain a group to itself, legitimate its deeds and aspirations, and provide important benchmarks for nonmembers trying to understand the group's cultural identity."[6]

Classic ethnographies in anthropology were all too often quasi-scientific reductions of a culture, guided by Western standards of cultural norms. Largely funded by government institutions, American anthropology became known as "salvage ethnography," the focus of which was to preserve a quickly disappearing past. The realization of how that past informed the present, and constructed a possible future, was of little concern. The voices of the people were subverted in the text, and concern with narrative was largely left to the folklorists.[7] Our work seeks to reflect on how narratives, rituals, and historical and collective memories function as a human wall of resistance to annihilation and a means to ensure survival.

Culture is a social construct that is usually understood in and through the contents of its traditions—its feelings, modes of action, forms of language, aspirations, interpersonal relations, images, ideas, and ideals. For example, Vera Schwarcz notes that the Hebrew word for "tradition" (Masoret) connotes the effort involved in the passing on of communal memories. Behind the noun, one finds the verb "to transmit." This verb can be traced to the Akkadian word *musaru*, which suggests two ideas:

the grasping of an object and the setting free of something.[8] Thus, tradition reveals a variety of contents: doctrine, stories, myths, creeds, symbols, experiences, and everyday moral decisions. Cultural memory represents another such carrier of the tradition.

> . . . never fight against memory. Even if it is painful, it will help you: it will give you something, it will enrich you. Ultimately, what would culture be without memory? What would philosophy be without memory? What would love be . . .? One cannot live without it. One cannot exist without remembrance.[9]

Tradition and Cultural Memory

From generation to generation, traditions pass on a world of meaning. Traditions carry the personal as well as communal experiences of a people: its implicit and explicit understandings, myths, stories, affectivities—anything that actualizes the potential of the human person. As Charles Davis states:

> A tradition is a way of responding to reality, including feelings, memories, images, ideas, attitudes, interpersonal relationships: in brief, the entire complex that forms life within a particular world, a world bounded by a horizon that determines the particular sense of reality that pervades it.[10]

Tradition also has two distinct parts: (1) the process—the *traditio,* the actual handing on, and (2) the product—the *traditium,* the content. In other words, tradition can be seen as both a participle, "remembering," and a noun, "remembrance" or "memory." "Remembrance is a particular form of action. If well cultivated, memorial acts may even strengthen the heart in moments of difficult transition."[11] In fact, participle and noun represent two sides of the same coin.

The same two elements can be found in cultural memory: it is both a remembering and a remembrance or memory. One side of cultural memory is the *traditio,* the process. Who remembers? It is a people, a society, a culture that carries a memory. How is it remembered? It is remembered in memory, raised in celebration, passed on orally, recorded in writings, designated to a sacred place. The other side is the *traditium,* the product. What is being remembered? What does this memory do? What does it

TABLE 1.1. Tradition: A what and how of transmitting cultural memory

TRADITIO		TRADITIUM	
Process		Content	
(Participle = Remembering)		(Noun = Remembrance)	
WHO REMEMBERS?	HOW IS IT REMEMBERED		WHAT DOES IT EVOKE?
—a people	—in memory		—feelings, biases
—a society	—in celebration		—modes of action
—a culture	—orally		—forms of language
	—in writings		—aspirations
			—interpersonal relations
			—images, ideas, ideals

evoke? What are its manifestations? What is remembered or evoked in-cludes feelings or affectivities, modes of action, forms of language, aspira-tions, interpersonal relations, images, ideas, ideals, and so forth. These ele-ments and more may be contained in a memory (Table 1.1). Traditions also reflect a variety of theological typologies, as Charles Davis makes clear.

In Table 1.1, the dynamics of the culture concept and the manner in which it is transmitted across generations is depicted. Memory becomes important as a survival mechanism when it becomes part of artistic, emo-tionally laden ways of forming group identity and meanings. This inher-ently creative process of being human accounts for the many unique ways that cultures have constructed themselves to understand reality and to pass on the important insights from generation to generation. It is crucial to this argument that the content of memory is biased by the language of the people, and that it is through language that the memory imposes the essential feelings that transmit that emotionally based message. As we discuss below, the very basis of human knowledge is the result of finely tuned emotional structures.

Understanding Cultural Memory

Cultural memory bears similarities to both historical memory and myth. "History is," as Carl Becker notes, "the memory of things said and done."[12]

History is constructed partially from the accounts of witnesses and partially from primary documents that reveal the memories of those involved in the events. We insist, however, that historical memory is a reconstruction of culturally relative "facts" that is always influenced by particular worldviews. Michel Foucault, for example, alerts us to the concepts of historically influenced processes that often masquerade as "facts," and need to be deconstructed. For this reason, we ground the following chapters in the historical context experienced by these communities.

Like historical memory, cultural memory is rooted in actual events and in the surrounding and resulting alignment of images, symbols, and affectivities that turn out to be even more persuasive than "facts." Many kinds of historical memories are transmitted through texts, oral history, tradition, plays, and memory. As Herbert Hirsch writes, these memories are not necessarily orderly or linear:

> In attempting to reconstruct our own history from what Lander . . . calls the "ruins of memory," we should be aware of the fact that what we come up with is composed partially of remembered experiences, partially of events that we have heard about that may be part of a family or group mythology, partially of images that we have recreated from a series of family remembered events. Historians and philosophers agree that personal recollections are used to formulate both the individual and the collective past. It is an attempt to chronicle human events remembered by human beings. History is moved by a series of social forces, including economics, religion, and institutions, mainly political, technological, ideological, and military. Just as historians create memory as they write history, as I write about memory, I am constructing a way to think about memory and history, and am consequently creating a paradigm, a way of thinking used to analyze and interpret some phenomenon.[13]

Occasionally, there are *historical memories that are so overwhelmingly significant that they define the essence of a people and become imperative for their survival.* Such is the case with the Holocaust. As Judith Miller says, "The Holocaust . . . makes sense only bit by bit—only if we try to encounter it one story, one memory, at a time."[14] Thus, the Jewish people exclaim, "Never again!" They will survive meaningfully only as long as the historical memory of the Holocaust remains active and alive. According to the theologian Abraham Joshua Heschel, this unwillingness to sever the cord of memory accounts for the spiritual survival of Jews in our time:

Why did our hearts throughout the ages turn to Eretz Israel, to the Holy Land? Because of memory. There is a slow and silent stream, a stream not of oblivion but of memory, from which we constantly drink before entering the realm of faith. To believe is to remember. The substance of our very being is memory, our way of living is retaining reminders, articulating memory.[15]

The *power* of cultural memory rests in the *conscious* decision to choose particular memories, and to give those memories precedence in communal remembrance.

Cultural memory, like myth,[16] has a historical basis, and, like myth, it can be transformative. Myths are powerful vehicles for transmitting historically rooted events, and they carry enormous amounts of cultural memory. Our own North American myths swirl around stories of George Washington and the Revolutionary War and the cultural memories of individualism. As a way of infusing our particular understanding of cultural memory with the sense of the sacred, we draw on the understanding of myth, or story, offered by Wendy Doniger O'Flaherty, who argues that

> a myth is a story that is sacred to and shared by a group of people who find their most important meanings in it; it is a story believed to have been composed in the past about an event in the past, . . . an event that continues to have meaning in the present because it is remembered; it is a story that is part of a larger group of stories.[17]

Suggesting that a story is sacred immediately throws us into questions of religious meaning: questions about life and death, divine intervention, creation, human nature, culture, ultimate meaning. Religious and psychosocial themes are difficult to separate from cultural memory because the private and the public realms are closely intertwined. The transforming characteristic of meaning attributed to myth is also characteristic of what is carried on in the process of cultural memory. Thus, *cultural memory transmits an experience rooted in history that has reached a culturally definitive, potentially transformative status.* As such, the myth/story of Guadalupe not only is a "master symbol . . . [because] it enshrines the major hopes and aspirations of an entire society,"[18] but it also has transformative potential as well.

Cultural memory may emerge from a catastrophic tragedy. In fact, many cultural memories often arise out of events that prove transformative, igniting recognizable shifts in the world of meaning for a people.

Whether cultural memory fulfills the need to transcend certain events or to maintain a corporate identity, it passes from generation to generation through oral traditions, written accounts, images, rituals, and dramas. It is evoked around image, symbol, affect, or event precisely because it keeps alive and transforms those events of the past. They are not bound or limited to the past, but continue to give meaning to the present.

How to Begin

For this study, it is particularly important to begin with a grounding in the Judeo-Christian tradition for three specific reasons: (1) It is a well-documented and well-researched tradition; (2) it has been integrated and interpreted for centuries by a variety of diverse cultures; and (3) it has had a powerful influence on the cultures that we present in this book. The very foundational struggle for existence that produced the culture known as the Hebrew people, as well as the many configurations of the Christian cultures, provides a rich area to mine for clues as to how memory is formed and molded, and how it is both functional as well as creative. Furthermore, although this seemingly Western bias could be called into question as part of our methodology, we will demonstrate that the apparent hegemony of this Judeo-Christian tradition has been reinvented, at times subverted, and never taken as the only "right way" to see the world. Christian concern for memory is ultimately rooted in the rabbinical traditions as preserved through the ages by the synagogue. Christianity inherited Judaism's memorial character, but centered its memory on the incarnation, life, death, and resurrection of Jesus. Eduardo Hoornaert notes that the peculiar character of the Christian memory throughout the course of history "is that of the defeated and the humbled, the marginalized and the condemned"[19] and is therefore not recorded in a history composed in the hegemonic historiographical tradition of great cultures, by way of discourses, monuments, archives, documents, iconography, and architecture.

> On the contrary, the Christian memory of the humbled is transmitted from generation to generation as a popular culture, an oral tradition, a cultural resistance. Hence, this Christian memory survives primarily in communities. Part and parcel of this tradition of struggle for an authentic Christian memory are the current practices of the base communities . . . Christian memory is by no means an individual memory . . . it is a collective memory . . . a memory of a people . . . defining the consciousness of a social group.[20]

In subsequent chapters, then, we present the following elements of cultural memory:

1. The establishment of identity, especially as it relates to the concept of ethnicity

2. The ability to reconstruct the past in order to exist in a meaningful manner in the present

3. Enculturation, that is, the manner in which being of an ethnic identity is learned and transmitted from generation to generation

4. Structures of transmission, which are the core of this endeavor and the key institutional mode by which memory is conveyed, be it image, narrative, rituals, or syncretism modes

5. The obligations connected to the groups' values that continue to ensure resiliency in the world today. Or, to put it another way, the moral imperatives that create the ideal humans for a particular culture.

6. Reflexivity, or the conscious ability to ground the everyday with the interpretation of the meta-memory

In the following chapters, we address how each of the above is integrated by the particular culture. Our historical-anthropological-theological methodology of image, narrative, ritual, and syncretism as they apply to Mexican Americans, Yaqui Indians, El Salvadorians, and Tzeltal Indians is intended to illuminate four manners of holding a meta-memory in a privileged position and articulating how that then becomes a beacon of meaning and of resistance for an ethnic group. We are in no way implying that these four "ways" are the sole means of conveying these structures. Rather, they are illustrative of ways of understanding the complexity of the phenomena of memory and culture.

2. The Power of Image
OUR LADY OF GUADALUPE

Here it is told. *Nican Mopohua*

OUR LADY OF GUADALUPE is a religious experience, but, of course, contemporary Mexican American devotees of Our Lady of Guadalupe do not enjoy a firsthand vision of her. Yet from their faith stories, it is undeniable that there is an encounter, a presence, and a relationship between them and La Virgen de Guadalupe. It is a vibrant daily occurrence. Even when this is not the case, the Guadalupe apparition is a primordial experience kept alive in the cultural memory of the community. This cultural memory is concretized in the Guadalupe image prominently displayed in many of her devotees' homes. By retelling the story of the Guadalupe's apparition and by their devotion, Mexican Americans share in the memory of the primordial experience. Some internalize this memory so that it becomes for them a personal religious experience, and to the degree in which that memory is faithful, it becomes a primordial experience.

This cultural memory is contained in the image of the Guadalupe itself; it is recorded in the Nahuatl document entitled *Nican Mopohua* (*Here It Is Told*).[1] Like all memories, cultural memory is a living and dynamic reality. The memory of the Guadalupe is recorded and transmitted in the stories her devotees narrate, in their devotional practices in her honor, in the naming of their children after her, and in their celebrations of her feast. Remembering and transmitting the Guadalupe experience is mainly a matter of affirming aspirations and nurturing the hope and strength needed to maintain one's identity.

The Guadalupe story appears to be a simple one, yet it is rooted in a sociopolitical and cultural history. We are grateful to the Benedictine sisters of Guadalupe Christo Rey in Mexico who initiated us into this story within a larger story. Their deep devotion to Our Lady of Guadalupe and their understanding of the lived reality of the poor was an immense contribution to grasping the power of this image. To facilitate an understanding of Guadalupe, those who promote her story and image usually begin with the time before the arrival of the Spaniards to Mexico.[2]

Historical Context

The account of the Guadalupe story, as regularly narrated by the Benedictine sisters, begins with Mexico's popular religious history.[3] It highlights the fact that the Mexican people are descendants of the pre-Columbian Olmec, who founded the first important civilization in Mexico around 1200 BCE. Because of their abiding influence on the other cultures of the region, the Olmec are considered the source of the Mesoamerican cultures. Through commerce and religion, the Olmec exercised a deep influence on the cultures of the Toltec, the Teotihuacans, the Maya, the Aztec, and the Zapotec, just to name a few. Toward the end of the twelfth and the beginning of the thirteenth century CE, seven Nahuatl tribes came to the valley of Mexico, one of which was the Aztec. The Aztec came from the northwest of Mexico, the land that is known as the mythic Aztlan. The people came under the leadership of their chief priest, Tenoch. According to legend, the gods told the priest that the people would see a sign indicating that they had reached the "Promised Land." The sign was an eagle perched on a nopal cactus with a serpent in its beak. This sign was reportedly found in the middle of seven lakes, and, as is well known, Mexico City is built upon these lakes.

During the reign of Montezuma I, the Aztec Empire was consolidated and its borders were expanded so that by 1502 CE, when Montezuma II was chosen emperor, the frontiers of the empire extended as far north as Sinaloa in present-day Mexico and as far south as Nicaragua, spanning, east to west, the Atlantic to the Pacific coast.

What we find in the telling and retelling of the story of Guadalupe is a reclaiming of the greatness of the past, a past whose inception and definition was initiated by the divine. The Aztec prospered in commerce, arts, and architecture. They built immense temples on the principal island of Tenochtitlan. On this island alone there were seventy-two temples. About 80,000 people inhabited the two islands of Tenochtitlan and Tlatelolco, which were connected by several land causeways and two aqueducts. On the smaller of the two islands stood Tlatelolco, a great cultural and commercial center, which, after the Spanish Conquest, would become a center for Catholic evangelization and learning.

In addition to their exquisite music, art, and architecture, the Aztec also had a highly developed religion. They worshiped Quetzalcoatl (the Lord), along with Ipalnemohuani (a god known as both Father and Mother), Tonatiuh (the new sun), and Ometeotl (the Lord and Lady who are near and close to us). These names, which frequently appear in Nahuatl literature, express God's relationship not only with human beings but also with the cosmos. (By transmitting the story of Our Lady of Guadalupe, the narrators intend to remind the people of their glorious ancestry.)

All this history was destructively altered when Hernán Cortés conquered the Aztec and asked the king of Spain to send Franciscans to evangelize what they called New Spain. The Franciscans arrived in 1521 and began their work of evangelization, but this was done in a climate of violent oppression against the indigenous people. To the indigenous people, the conquest was a sign that their gods had been overthrown or had abandoned them. Nothing was left for them but to die. This is the context in which the story of Guadalupe emerges. In the midst of death and destruction, a great sign of hope and liberation appears—Guadalupe, the mother of the awaited fifth sun, the new Quetzalcoatl. Holy Mary of Guadalupe, the maternal face of God, the beloved Mother of God, comes to console a suffering people.

The Text and Its Story

The *Nican Mopohua*, transcribed from the oral language of Nahuatl, records the story of Our Lady of Guadalupe. Nahuatl is a highly symbolic language that conveys "much beyond words" and is "much more profound, more significant, much more rich and full than Indo-European languages. It is a simple language, direct, smooth, precise, elegant, resounding, beautiful, profound, highly significant, and even sublime."[4] An understanding of Nahuatl cultural symbols and myths is essential for interpreting the *Nican Mopohua* narrative. Two important aspects of the Nahuatl language are (1) the use of *disfracismos*—a way of communicating profound concepts by using two words or symbols instead of one; and (2) the use of numerology—the interpretation of numbers as having symbolic meaning; two numbers are particularly significant in the Nahuatl language and culture: the number four, which indicates completion, and the number five, which refers to the center of the world.

The *Nican Mopohua* text records Saturday, December 9, 1531, early in the morning, as the time of the apparition of Our Lady of Guadalupe to Juan Diego, the baptismal name of Cuahtlatoatzin (One Who Talks like an Eagle). In Nahuatl culture, *muy de madrugada* (very early in the morning) referred not only to daybreak but also to the beginning of all time. Thus, the image represents the beginning of something new, and the

Guadalupe event takes on the significance of a foundational experience equal in importance to the origin of the world and the cosmos.[5]

The apparition account relates that, on his way to church, Juan Diego hears music. In the context of Nahuatl *disfracismos*, music represented one-half of a dual way of expressing truth, beauty, philosophy, and divinity. Flower and song together manifested the presence of the divine. When Juan Diego hears such beautiful and enchanting music, he asks, "Have I gone into paradise? Can I be hearing what I am hearing?" The word *canto* ("song" or "music") appears five times. As mentioned above, in Nahuatl cosmology, five was a symbol for the center of the world.[6] The reference to *canto*, then, points to another way of experiencing, understanding, and conceptualizing contact with the divine. Similarly significant in the Nahuatl account is the use of the number four, which symbolized cosmic totality or completion. In the text, Juan Diego asks four questions: First, "Am I worthy to hear what I am hearing? Perhaps I am dreaming?" Second, "I must awake from this dream. Where am I?" Third, "Have I perhaps entered the land of paradise that our ancient ones have told us about?" Finally, "Am I in heaven?" There is a moment of silence between the time Juan Diego hears the music and asks the questions. This silence, in conjunction with the nighttime, represents another dual Nahuatl expression that serves to link the event with the origins of creation.[7]

Upon hearing the music, Juan Diego looks to the east, the home of the sun and symbol of God. The sun rises in the east, the direction from which Guadalupe appears. Again, Guadalupe enters the Nahuatl reality in a way that the people can understand. She first addresses Juan Diego by the diminutive form of his name, which in Spanish is translated as Juan Dieguito—a Nahuatl form of expression conveying maternal love, delicacy, and reverence.[8] The *Nican Mopohua* does not emphasize Guadalupe's apparition to Juan Diego but rather his "encounter" with her. What is the nature of this encounter? There are two characters: Juan Diego and Our Lady of Guadalupe. Juan Diego, a fifty-two-year-old man, is a member of the oppressed and enslaved indigenous people. How does he perceive Our Lady of Guadalupe? He sees her as a woman of nobility. At this point, the text makes an important distinction. Our Lady of Guadalupe is standing up. Nobles, however, whether Aztec or Spanish, would receive people sitting down, sometimes on a pedestal or in some other specific, designated place. Such a posture was meant to show not only that the individual in question presided over the people but also, given the experience of the conquest, that such an individual had dominion over the people. In the case of Guadalupe, however, the nobility that Juan Diego observes in this woman is not of the dominant sort.[9] Unlike the conquistadors, Guadalupe does not treat Juan Diego as one of the conquered ones; on the contrary, she acknowledges and restores his dignity by her posture, the tone of her words, and her dialogue.

Guadalupe's presence also elicits a response from the earth. The flowers and the ground around her, the text reports, glow like gold. This encounter affects the world. Guadalupe, therefore, presents new life to the people and to the land. The text further describes the "Lady" as clothed with the radiance of the sun. In Nahuatl culture, a person's clothing, especially that of an important person, was dyed a certain color and adorned with objects or symbols that revealed who that person was, who had sent that person, or where that person had come from. The rays of sun emanating from behind Guadalupe informed the indigenous people, as represented by Juan Diego, that God formed part of her experience and personality.[10] Virgilio Elizondo puts it as follows: "The Sun god was the principal god in the native pantheon. . . . She is greater than the greatest of the native divinities, yet she does not do away with the Sun."[11]

One of the most important lines in the narrative is that in which Guadalupe reveals her identity: "Know and be assured, the smallest of my children, that I am the ever Virgin Mary, Mother of the true God through whom one lives, the creator on which all depends, Lord of the heavens and the earth."[12] Thus, Guadalupe identifies herself as: (1) Mother of God, who is the God of Truth; (2) Mother of the Giver of Life; (3) Mother of the Creator; (4) Mother of the One Who Makes the Sun and the Earth; and (5) Mother of the One Who Is Near. These titles coincide with names given to the ancient Aztec gods. She refers to five names of gods known to the Nahua; thus, Guadalupe states who she is and where she is from using Nahuatl duality and phrases.

The Virgin tells Juan Diego that she wants a temple to be built for her, where she can bestow her *love, compassion, help,* and *defense* on all those who come to her. She wishes her house to be at Tepeyac, a site of great significance.[13] Previously, it had been the shrine of Tonantzin, one of the major earth mother divinities of the Aztec people. One scholar argues that "it was very natural for the Aztec to associate Guadalupe with the pagan Tonantzin, since both were virgin mothers of gods and both appeared at the same place."[14] Yet several major differences are noted between Tonantzin and Guadalupe:

The Virgin of Guadalupe was not a mere Christian front for the worship of a pagan goddess. The adoration of Guadalupe represented a

profound change in Aztec religious belief. . . . Tonantzin was both
a creator and a destroyer. The nature and function of the Virgin of
Guadalupe are entirely different from those of the pagan earth goddess. The Christian ideals of beauty, love, and mercy associated with
the Virgin of Guadalupe were never attributed to the Aztec deity.
The functions of the Catholic Virgin are much broader and more
beneficial to man than those of the Aztec nature goddess. Guadalupe protects her children (the Mexicans) from harm, cures their
sicknesses, and aids them in all manner of daily undertakings.[15]

The text relates how Juan Diego, following the mandate of Guadalupe,
goes to the bishop, only to be told to come back at a more convenient
time. Juan Diego returns to Guadalupe and despondently addresses the
Virgin as "Señora, la más pequeña de mis hijas" (Lady, the most humble
of my daughters). By referring to the Virgin in this manner, he implies
that she, too, is poor and despised, just as he is. In turn, Juan Diego tells
the Virgin that he is the wrong messenger, and to send someone "who is
of greater importance, who is known, who is respected, and who is esteemed." The use of four terms to describe the ideal envoy represents, in
keeping with Nahuatl numerology, totality and completion. Juan Diego
believes that he is not taken seriously because he is an Indian and that her
mission would best be completed if a person of higher status were sent.

Juan Diego asks forgiveness from the Virgin for any pain he may have
caused her by his failure to convince the bishop of her message. Juan Diego believes that it is his fault that he was not accepted.[16] This sense of
self-deprecation and unworthiness reflects the tragic result of the conquest of the Nahuatl. The Virgin absolutely refuses to choose another
messenger. She reaffirms her desire that Juan Diego be her messenger,
although she has "many servants and messengers" from whom to choose.
She does not negate or deny the oppression that Juan Diego is experiencing, but she does "insist" on and "beg" for his involvement, using such
phrases as "Con rigor te mando"; "Te ruego"; and "Mucho te ruego" (I
firmly command you; I beg you; I entreat you very much).

The account seems to portray a conversation and dialogue between
equals. Yet Juan Diego is obsequious to the request of this remarkable
woman he has encountered. Guadalupe accords Juan Diego the dignity
and respect of a person who has the freedom to choose (Siller, 64–65).
She concludes her conversation with Juan Diego as follows: "And once
again, tell the bishop that I send you, the ever Virgin, Holy Mary, Mother
of God, it is she who sends you." In response, Juan Diego reaccepts and

reembraces this mission. His desire not to cause the Virgin any pain as well as his wish to make his commitment manifest are evident in his joyful and energetic response: "I will go and complete your order" (65).

Following this conversation, Juan Diego returns to the bishop's home in Mexico City. Once again, Juan experiences difficulties. He subjects himself to distrust, humiliation, and disbelief for the sake of the mission. When the bishop finishes interrogating Juan Diego, he states that he cannot build the temple on the Indian's word alone. He sends Juan Diego back to ask the Virgin for a sign.

Siller makes an interesting observation with regard to the communication between Juan Diego and the bishop (68–69). When Juan Diego is speaking with the bishop, he refers to the Virgin as the "always Virgin, Holy Mary, Mother of Our Savior the Lord Jesus Christ." Siller suggests that this is a theological reflection on the part of Juan Diego (69). Guadalupe never refers to herself as the "Mother of Our Savior the Lord Jesus Christ." Siller argues that with the return of the self (Juan Diego's restored dignity) comes the ability and perhaps the freedom to theologize. Or perhaps Juan Diego is wily and cunning enough to utilize terms and language that the bishop would easily grasp.

After agreeing to elicit a sign from the Lady so that the bishop may believe, Juan Diego returns home. When he arrives at his home, he finds that his uncle, Juan Bernardino, is sick. His uncle asks Juan Diego to go to Mexico City and bring back a priest to administer the last rites. Juan Diego finds himself caught in a dilemma. Is he to fulfill his uncle's request, or is he to meet the Lady in order to receive the sign? The issue of death is paramount. Juan Diego decides to go for a priest so that the last rites may be given:

> The sickness of the uncle came at a crucial moment in the mission of Juan Diego. . . . For us perhaps it would have been more important if the mother or father of Juan Diego was sick, . . . but for most of the Meso-American people, the uncle played a social role of capital importance. . . . The uncle received the maximum expression of respect that one could give an adult, and he was the critical element in understanding the barrio and the people. (76)

On his way to Mexico City, Juan Diego decides to take an alternate route so as not to have to "disappoint the Lady." However, as he is walking, he hears the Lady calling to him, asking him where he is going. Juan Diego is convinced that the sad news of his uncle's mortal illness will cause grief for the Virgin. He begins his conversation with her by saying, "I'm going to cause you affliction" (79). Guadalupe's response to Juan Diego's concern is expanded to include all sickness and anguish. She says, "No temas esa enfermedad, ni ninguna otra enfermedad y angustia" (Do not fear this sickness, or any other sickness or anguish; 82).

She continues with five questions (again, a reference to the center of the world): "Am I not here, your mother? Are you not under my shadow and protection? Am I not your fountain of life? Are you not in the folds of my mantle, in the crossing of my arms? Is there anything else that you need?" In these questions, Guadalupe reveals herself as someone with authority. For Mexicans, a person with authority was a person who had the ability to cast a shadow, precisely what Guadalupe does with her mantle: "Mexicans understand authority . . . as one who casts a large shadow . . . because the one who is greater than all the rest must shelter or protect the great and small alike" (83).

Juan Diego believes in Guadalupe's authority, and Juan Bernardino is cured, giving rise thereby to the Virgin's first miracle. However, a greater miracle occurs when the apparition of Guadalupe brings psychic healing for Juan Diego and ultimately for the Nahuatl people. The healing of the uncle extends to Juan, who "felt much consoled and was left feeling contented" (84). At peace with the knowledge that his uncle had been cured, Juan Diego asks the Virgin to send him, with a sign, to the bishop. The Virgin orders Juan Diego to go to the top of Tepeyac and look for roses to cut, gather, and bring to her. She touches the flowers and makes herself present in them, thus inserting herself within the symbolic logic of the Indians, for whom flowers signified truth and dignity (86–88).

Juan Diego, filled with faith and resolve, goes to the bishop's palace. There he encounters disrespect and ridicule from the courtiers, yet he holds his ground and waits to see the bishop. Siller makes another interesting observation to the effect that such a scene is quite common whenever an Indian or a poor person is placed in the power of the dominant culture. In this particular case, the servants at the bishop's palace try to take away what Juan Diego is holding in his *tilma* (cloak), but Guadalupe had ordered him not to show the flowers to anyone except the bishop.

Siller sees this attempt to take the flowers from Juan Diego as symbolic: it is an attempt on the part of the dominant culture to take away the Indians' truth. The conquerors and the dominant culture have already taken from Juan Diego and his people their land, their goods, their city, their form of government, and their reasons for being and acting. Now they want to take away Juan Diego's symbol of truth, that is, all he has left. Siller argues that, as a result of the Guadalupe event, it is no longer possible to take the truth away from the indigenous people (93). Rather, it is Juan Diego, an Indian, who brings the truth to the Spanish bishop.

After he is made to wait for a long time, the servants inform the bishop of Juan Diego's presence and allow him to enter. Again, Juan Diego relates his story. He implies that by doubting him and asking him for a sign, the bishop is in fact questioning and demanding a sign from the Virgin. In the text, Juan Diego says that the Virgin "sent me up to this hill to get flowers, but I knew it was not the season, yet I did not doubt." After this statement, Juan Diego hands over the proof, the roses, and asks the bishop to take them. As the flowers fall from Juan Diego's *tilma*, the fifth apparition occurs. The image of Guadalupe appears imprinted on the *tilma*. When the bishop and those around him see it, they all kneel, admire it, and repent for their failure to believe.

There is a given content to Guadalupe, not just whatever one wants to think about this event. Memory is carried in memory, just as a couple will never forget the beginnings of their relationship, yet their relationship changes over time. It is "cultural" because it has become embedded in the totality of the Mexican consciousness and continues to elicit meaning today. Memory does something about defining this culture. Carriers of culture put emphasis on the memory. This holding on to, passing on, and reinterpreting the memory is not only an intellectual process but also an affective one.

The practical fundamental theology of Johann Baptist Metz contends that memory can be an "expression of eschatological hope" and a "category of the salvation of identity."[17] He further states that "memory is . . . of central importance in any theory of history and society as a category of persistence to the passage of time."[18] This understanding and application of memory provides a model for grasping the impact of the Guadalupe event. Our Lady of Guadalupe represents an eschatological hope for those who believe in her (Table 2.1). For Hispanic/Latino Catholics, to uphold the memory of the Guadalupe event is to show "solidarity in memory with the dead and the conquered."[19]

To put it succinctly, cultural memory continues to exist because it feeds a basic need for identity, salvation, hope, and resistance to annihilation. The cultural memory of the Guadalupe event exists because there is a need for it. The story speaks of the restoration of human dignity in a voice once silenced and now restored. It speaks of the restoration of a lost language and a way of perceiving the divine. It speaks of accessing lost symbols and transforming them in a new time. Ultimately, it speaks and continues to speak of a shared experience of a people—a people who

TABLE 2.1. Cultural memory as manifested in Our Lady of Guadalupe

WHO?	HOW?	WHAT?
—A people carry a memory.	—image/story	—Feelings
—Memory is also a carrier	—celebration/song	—Aspirations
	—*Nican Mopohua*	—Devotion
	—Basilica of Guadalupe	—Direction
		—Hope

suffer. The Guadalupe event resurrected the Nahuatl cultural memory at a time when everything in the world of the Nahuatl people had been destroyed. By activating their cultural memory, Our Lady of Guadalupe empowered and renewed the life of that people.

What characteristics of Nahuatl cultural memory does the Guadalupe story activate? The following points from the story should be particularly noted in this regard. First, Guadalupe speaks not in the language of the conquistadors (Spanish) but rather in the language of the conquered, the oppressed, the marginalized, and the silenced (Nahuatl). Second, when she appears, she presents herself in the symbols of the people. She thus uses the symbols of the marginalized and at the same time transforms them. Third, by utilizing the names of the gods of the Nahuatl people, she identifies herself as *uno de ellos* (one of them). Consequently, Guadalupe calls forth the cultural memory of the people by entering into their history and incarnating their culture, symbols, and language. In so doing, she validates them and gives them a place in the world. She dialogues with them and thus empowers them. She restores their dignity and facilitates their liberation by demanding that they participate in the reclaiming of their own voice. She shows "solidarity in memory with the dead and the conquered." This process of empowerment is played out in the person of Juan Diego, who represents the oppressed people.

Today, the image of Guadalupe pervades the neighborhoods of over twelve million people of Mexican descent in the United States, whether as a statue or a painting in a sacred corner of the home or as an image on T-shirts, on the sides of buildings, and even on business logos. Her name, Guadalupe, is not only bestowed by parents on their children, both girls and boys, but also given to parishes and churches, streets and towns, rivers and mountains.

A deeper appreciation of the Guadalupe story as cultural memory can be gained through the analysis of Clodomiro Siller, a Mexican priest, theologian, and anthropologist. Siller combines his academic work in anthropology with extensive pastoral work among the indigenous peoples of Mexico.[20] His anthropological interests in indigenous peoples, particularly those who speak Nahuatl, and his theological work are based on liberation theology.[21] The primary reason for using Siller's work is that he is among the very few who have attempted to understand the Guadalupe event from the viewpoint of the indigenous Nahua rather than the perspective of those who are too quick to Christianize the event. What follows, therefore, is a close reading of the narrative of the apparition with particular emphasis on its meaning within sixteenth-century Nahuatl culture.

According to Siller, an attempt to read the narrative with a Judeo-Christian mentality would render it false.[22] Such a reading would impose a preconceived meaning on the symbols and, as a result, neglect the unique symbolic universe of the Nahuatl people. The Nahua themselves must function as the principal spokespersons for telling other cultures about Nahuatl culture. As is true in all cultures, Nahuatl myths help determine the meaning and significance of their cultural symbols. These become multivalent over time. The flower, for example, represents truth, beauty, and authenticity for the Nahua. Thus, Nahuatl mythology holds that the truth of all things was brought by the god Quetzalcoatl in the form of a flower so that humanity could live happily.

Sources of the Narrative

Our Lady of Guadalupe appeared in 1531, ten years after the Spanish Conquest. Because her appearance dates from well before the age of newspapers and the mass media, it contrasts radically with other reported appearances of Christian images, such as that of Lourdes, where the story was immediately carried around the world by rail and steamship. Further, Guadalupe emerged in a society with an enormous language divide. At Lourdes, everyone spoke the same language, and all pilgrims recited one and the same story, which revolved around the well-known grotto by the river. At Tepeyac, however, a whole world separated the Indians, who thought in terms of Tonantzin (Our Mother) and their own traditions, and the Spaniards, who thought in terms of the old Marian shrine of Guadalupe in Extremadura (Spain), a well at the base of the hill, and of other ancient Marian shrines of Europe as well as the entire Catholic tradition regarding the Virgin.

Although there are different positions with regard to the existence of an oral tradition of the Guadalupe event, there is evidence that such a tradition did indeed exist, including Juan Diego's own testimony, for as long as seventeen years after the event itself.[23]

> From Indian to Indian, from community to community, the word spread. What had happened to Juan Diego at Mount Tepeyac began to be told, along with his adventures in Mexico City, how the Virgin had cured his uncle, and the other marvels that took place in the presence of the Virgin of Guadalupe. Rapidly, the deeds began to enter the traditions of the people.[24]

In addition, the appearance of Our Lady of Guadalupe in 1531 is recorded in an ancient document entitled *Nican Mopohua*, a copy of which Rodríguez was able to examine in the course of on-site research in March 1986 at the Institute for Guadalupan Studies in Mexico City. The oldest copy of the *Nican Mopohua* was written sometime between 1540 and 1545 by the learned Indian convert Antonio Valeriano.[25] It should be pointed out, however, that some scholars date this report much later, as late as the seventeenth century (1649), and attribute its authorship to Luis Lasso de la Vega, a chaplain at the shrine at Tepeyac.[26]

In the first volume of the *Monumentos Guadalupanos*, there are two ancient copies of the Guadalupan account written by Antonio Valeriano. The paper is literally worn away in many places, especially the first page. The second copy, dated about forty years after the first, toward the end of the sixteenth century, is written in a far more careful literary style.[27] The earlier version has a spelling and writing style that is characteristic of the mid-sixteenth century. In addition, the vocabulary, language, sentence structure, and idioms of the two documents are different. The earlier document is written in a literary style that reflects the way the Indians spoke at the time.[28] The text used here is the one translated into Spanish by Don Primo Feliciano Velázquez in 1926.

Rereading of the Text

A text is true to the extent that it leads one toward further meaning. In this section, the meaning of the text/narrative will be discussed. The apparition narrative of Our Lady of Guadalupe in the *Nican Mopohua* begins with the historical context of the event. The text reveals that the woman, the Virgin Mary, Mother of God, appeared in the setting of the *post guerra* (1531), ten years after the final conquest of the Aztec Empire by the Spaniards in 1521. Our Lady of Guadalupe appeared to Juan Diego at Tepeyac in what is today the northern part of Mexico City. At the time of the apparition, the Aztec nation had been subordinated into a state of alienation, suffering, and oppression.

Guadalupe reveals herself as coming from "El verdadero Dios por quien se vive" (The true God through whom one lives). In Nahuatl, this phrase served as the name of one of the gods. When the Virgin states that she is from the one true God, the God who gives life, the Nahua would have recognized this god to be their god.[29] Moreover, Guadalupe's self-designation as "always Virgin" is Nahuatl for *doncella entera*, or "whole woman," in Spanish. Virginity was highly valued in Nahuatl culture by both men and women. Consequently, they would have looked upon Our Lady of Guadalupe as an embodiment of a preconquest value of their culture.[30] Thus, her image represents values esteemed by the Nahua themselves. This is the story and the image that has been passed on for generations. This holding on to such a dramatic event has preserved indigenous elements that were the foci of repression and eradication. It has also persisted as the source of a deeply felt worldview in which hope and faith, in the face of incredible devastation, can still find truth.

Theological Insights

What theological insights can be derived from this cultural memory of Our Lady of Guadalupe? To begin with, we would argue that Our Lady of Guadalupe represents far more than just compassion, relief, and a means for reconciliation between the sixteenth-century Spanish and the indigenous peoples. In fact, Virgilio Elizondo has already identified at least four powerful theological interpretations of this drama.[31]

First, by identifying herself as "Mother of the true God through whom one lives," Guadalupe identifies herself with the supreme creative power.[32]

Second, Guadalupe is a symbol of a new creation, a new people: "Only in an event that clearly originated in heaven could the conquest and rape of the people of Mexico be reversed and a people be truly proud of their new existence."[33]

Third, Guadalupe responds to the deepest instincts of the Mexican psyche, which Elizondo identifies as an obsession with legitimacy, that is, anxiety about being an orphaned people.[34] One could go so far as to say that the drama addresses a deeper need for dignity, for restoration of self—a self made in the image and likeness of the Creator. Perhaps most significantly, Guadalupe also suggests that the deeper need is to experience the maternal face of God.

Fourth, Guadalupe symbolizes a reversal of power: "The reversal of power was not done through military force . . . but through the penetration of symbols whose core meaning is somewhat mutually understood."[35]

To these interpretations we can add the following four theological and anthropological insights. The first is that God does care. Theologically, one would say God is faithful to the covenant that promises that God is *our* God and that we are God's people. Guadalupe constitutes a further manifestation of that promise of God. Johann Baptist Metz writes: "Christian faith can be understood as an attitude according to which man [sic] remembers promises that have been made and hopes that are experienced as a result of those promises and commits himself [sic] to those memories."[36] Such is precisely the case with the devotees of Guadalupe. Through the process that carries cultural memory, the people remember the promises of compassion, help, and defense that Guadalupe has made. Because these promises have been made, the people experience hope—a hope carried through cultural memory. As a result of these promises, the people commit themselves to the Guadalupan memory and image—that which can be read, touched, felt, seen, experienced.

The second insight is that Guadalupe represents a symbol of death and resurrection. In many ways she frees each person to die to the old, destructive, and painful life and to believe in new life. When giving presentations on Guadalupe, Rodríguez suggests to her audience that if they are unable to remember a time in their lives when they felt as if they were nothing, they will never be able to understand the Guadalupan story. In other words, we must remember where we came from, that we are dust, that we were slaves in Egypt, that we were oppressed, and that God has carried us and will continue to carry us to freedom. Cultural memory seals in our minds the stories of those who sought to control and dominate and of those who led the struggle for liberation.

The third insight has to do with the example of God, who, in order to enter into a divine-human dialogue, was willing to take on human form. In the same way, Guadalupe enters into the Nahuatl world, the Mexican world, the Mexican American world, the world of those who call out to her, believe in her, and trust in her. She comes in a way that the people readily understand—clothed in their symbols and embodying their identity. She accesses and resurrects a memory in cultural stories and truths.

She meets the people where they are and leads them to a deeper wisdom. She makes use of their symbols, and leads them beyond them.

The fourth and final insight is that Guadalupe's message of love and compassion, help and protection, cannot be frozen into a mere devotional experience. Rather, the message has to do with the affirmation of a people. Ultimately, the drama speaks of unconditional love and a place in salvation history.[37] Her image is a carrier of eschatological hope insofar as the people visit her, look upon her, and know that everything will be fine. Such knowledge, however, does not mean that nothing further is expected of them. On the contrary, she hears, affirms, heals, and enables them. Part of the healing, therefore, is a call for them to stand up for themselves.

There is so much more that could be passed on about this story, about the significance of affectivity, about carriers of culture. However, given the constraints of the present chapter, we wish to conclude with the following two comments. First, a quotation from poet Baba Dioum that is very much to the point: "In the end what will endure is what we love, and what we love is what we understand, and what we understand we are taught."[38] It is our hope that the message and image of the power and the healing of Our Lady of Guadalupe will continue to be loved, understood, and taught. Second, although we have identified and described an image that speaks to a depth experience remembered and mediated within Mexican American culture, the Christian tradition is ample enough to be cross-cultural. Unfortunately, efforts to be Christian have in many ways been attempts to eliminate other cultures. Yet it is clear that the image of Guadalupe not only lies within Christian culture but also reclaims and honors the culture of the Mexican American. What would happen if Christianity began to reclaim other cultural traditions—such as the Celtic, the African, and the Caribbean—that have been similarly eliminated? Perhaps then our brothers and sisters would no longer feel like aliens in the Promised Land.

Theologies are not pure, uncontaminated intellectual enterprises; they are influenced by a variety of interests. They cannot be intelligently studied apart from other writings coming out of the same tradition taken as a whole. To make complete sense, they have to be contextualized in the economic, social, political, and artistic life of the social groups from which they sprang.[39]

In other words, we are all influenced by experience. Each person is the product of a complex of experiences collected over a lifetime. When a person or a people have had a significant or depth experience, it is often embodied and expressed in a symbol. The symbol can pull together all the aspects of one's life and elevate the experience to an encounter with the divine. Within the Mexican American Catholic experience, the image of Our Lady of Guadalupe functions as such a symbol. The cultural memory of the Guadalupe event is a dynamic, diachronic carrier of meaning, symbolized in her image. Through her story, image, and affective influence, she carries, by means of cultural memory, the religious-cultural tradition of the Mexican American people. From generation to generation, the cultural memory of Guadalupe tells Mexican Americans who they are and to whom they belong.

A theology that raises questions of truth, meaning, and affectivity is imperative for understanding the power behind the story of Our Lady of Guadalupe. Her story has threefold significance. First, it serves as the foundation of Mexican Christianity: that is, a blending of Christianity with indigenous understanding. Second, it provides a connection between the indigenous and the Spanish cultures.[40] And finally, the story anchors and supports an example of cultural memory, an unexplored dimension that will be further developed in this book.

The Significance of Guadalupe

During her early work on Guadalupe, Jeanette Rodríguez sought to make credible the insights of Mexican American women and to place on the theological table the discussion of Guadalupe as a credible theological source. Discourse about her is significant not only in the category of popular religion, but in those of revelation and grace as well.

Recently, in a PBS interview, noted religious scholar Huston Smith stated that Christianity's true meaning is expressed in "a living conversation between the human and the divine that goes on generation after generation." Smith's insight resonated with conversations between Rodríguez and Guadalupe devotees, who also assume an active and living conversation with Guadalupe. This conversation is passed on from generation to generation, from parent to child, from catechist to believer, from teacher to student, from sister to sister, from brother to brother. Cognitively, the significance of Guadalupe is that she responds to the deepest desires of the Mexican psyche; her iconography contains symbols that the indigenous encountered, understood, and honored.

The titles Guadalupe used to introduce herself in the official account of the *Nican Mopohua*—Mother of God, who is the God of Truth; Mother of the Giver of Life; Mother of the Creator; Mother of the One Who Makes the Sun and the Earth; Mother of the One Who Is Near—coincide with the names given the ancient Mexican gods.[41] The five names of the gods were well known to the Nahua. Guadalupe stated who she was and where she came from utilizing what the Nahua understood to be the operative essence as well as the cosmological and historical dimensions of their gods. In a quiet, gentle manner, she enters into the ordinary experiences of the people. Affectively, the woman who speaks touches the deepest beliefs and longings of the human heart: the desire and need to be seen, heard, understood, accepted, embraced, and loved. As the poet John Donahue explained, "Unless you see someone in the light of love, you don't see them at all."[42] By identifying herself as "Mother of the true God through whom one lives," Guadalupe connects herself with the supreme creative power. She is a sign of a new creation, a new people.[43]

The drama of Guadalupe addresses a deep need for dignity and restoration of self—a self that reflects the image and likeness of the Creator. The Guadalupe encounter speaks of unconditional love and a people's place in salvific history. Perhaps most significantly, it affirms a need to experience the wholeness of God in the face of patriarchal imperialism.

As an aspect of the face of God that is often associated with the maternal—love, compassion, help, and defense—Guadalupe hears and heals all the people's laments, miseries, and sufferings. Initially, she does not bring her presence or message to the center of power and domination, but to the poor and abandoned. As the God of Abraham and Sara once did, she makes her stand with the "vanquished." To the oppressed she brings a spirit of hope in the presentation of the roses to Juan Diego at a time of coldness and barrenness. Her presence is ushered in with music that he hears as he approaches. This encounter sustains the logical symbolic culture of the Indian, since for the Nahua, flower and song together manifest the presence of the divine.

How is this message of 1531 transmitted to us today in the first decade of the twenty-first century? Wherever there are crucified peoples and pharaohs standing on the necks of the oppressed, there will be a need to hear the significant message of Guadalupe. From the midst of the poor (personified in Juan Diego) comes our call to conversion and faith. To believe in Guadalupe is to believe in the poor and the God who stands among them. Let us examine more closely the message, then and now (Table 2.2).

The Guadalupe message then and now calls for a response: a response of faith, conversion, and participatory transformation. The encounter is

TABLE 2.2. The Guadalupe message: Then and now

THE SIGNIFICANCE OF THE GUADALUPE MESSAGE—1531	THE SIGNIFICANCE OF THE GUADALUPE MESSAGE—2005
a. Calls for the restoration of the dignity of the indigenous people dominated by the Spanish Conquest of present-day Mexico	a. Calls for the restoration of the dignity of those crushed by sustained domination and oppression in whatever form it takes: intrapsychic (i.e., internal anxieties, conflicts, doubts), interpersonal, political, social, religious, gender, sexual orientation
b. Sought to overturn the indigenous experience from one of destruction and death due to the conquest to one of participation in a new world that gives life and freedom to all	b. Seeks to overturn, change, challenge those contexts of destruction and death due to sustained oppression in the hopes of contributing to a world that gives life and freedom to all
c. Introduced the mediation of an ordinary layperson, Juan Diego (who, in this case, represents a people who are dying), who played an irreplaceable role as one who ushered in a new order for Church and society	c. Challenges the Juan Diegos among ordinary laypersons/women/minorities to usher in a new order for Church and society

Source: Benedictine sisters of Guadalupe, Cuernavaca, Mexico, personal communication, 1996.

a transhistorical moment in which God, who is both father and mother, addresses the devotees and encourages their hearts to be moved toward healing, reconciling, sustaining, and loving.

The Guadalupe event is rooted in history. It has a given content. From the onset of her work on Guadalupe, Rodríguez identified Guadalupe as a cultural memory. Cultural memory is contained in the image of Guadalupe itself; it is recorded in the Nahuatl document entitled *Nican Mopohua* (*Here It Is Told*). Memories are not limited to the written word. They live and are expressed in a historical reality. The memory of Guadalupe is carried and transmitted in the stories the people share, in the devotions that express their faith in her, and in their celebrations of her. Their remembering and evoking is mainly a matter of feelings and aspirations, of searching for hope and strength. A memory like Guadalupe is carried by a people in their historical, social, and political world. This memory of Guadalupe passes on the values of self-worth and appreciation of one's own language, culture, and tradition. The image and message of

Guadalupe, therefore, are vehicles for cultural memory. As cultural memory, Guadalupe evokes an affectivity that bonds individuals not only to her but to each other, thus becoming a key element in the calling together of a community of people, "un pueblo" (Figure 2.1). This grasping of, passing on, and reinterpreting the memory is both an intellectual and an affective process.

The cultural memory of the Guadalupe event continues to exist after the historical moment because it continues to inform the need for identity, hope, and resistance to the external forces that work to annihilate difference. The Guadalupe story speaks of the restoration of human dignity

FIGURE 2.1. Contemporary tattoo of Our Lady of Guadalupe, Blood Reserve, Canada

in a voice once silenced and now reestablished. This dignity and voice are restored through a faith claim that both connects with the "other" and challenges us to a more inclusive openness regarding the revelation of God and the complexity of being human.

In the Hebrew scriptures, God is faithful to the covenant with a people once caught in slavery by dominant powers—a covenant that repeatedly affirms the people's relationship with an eminent and loving God. Similarly, Guadalupe also reflects this biblical covenant. Guadalupe appears, remains present, and promises to respond to one's suffering, misery, and lamentations when one calls upon her, trusts her, and loves her.

Her message reminds all oppressed and marginalized people that the manifestation of the divine takes a stand with them and shows them love, compassion, help, and defense. The Guadalupe event, memory, and story recall who Mexicans are as a people, how they have been oppressed, and how God sides with all the poor and calls us all to liberation and healing.[44]

3. The Power of Secrecy and Ceremony
YAQUI RESISTANCE AND SPIRITUALITY

I N THE EARLY EVENING, as the hot desert air slowly cooled, we gathered with the Yaqui in their dirt-floored temple. Women with shawls over their heads sat toward the back, men toward the front of the building. Everything about the structure seemed from another era: the whitewashed adobe, crudely repaired in places; its rustic look; the array of icons and statues. The drumming was slow and rhythmic, the people, serious and focused. The Maestro began the song, and the women, with the ends of their shawls covering their mouths, responded in chant. It is a chant style that is heard today wherever Indians gather, that seemingly tonal mantra that is part of the spirit tradition. However, as we sat and listened, we suddenly realized that the chants were real words, and they were in Latin—a Latin neither of us had ever heard. Rather, it was an ancient Latin of the sort taught in the sixteenth century. And here, in the contemporary Yaqui village of Guadalupe, Arizona, five hundred years of time were swept away.

Yaqui Cosmology: An Etic[1] Interpretation

In this chapter, we approach the enigma of memory in a manner that highlights the power of culture as an organizer of resistance. We find the case study of the Yaqui to be one of special interest precisely because of their structures for enculturating secrecy that resist forces of assimilation. "Trained observers," writes the historian Thomas R. McGuire, "invariably argue that Yaquis have successfully battled repeated attempts . . . to destroy their ritual expressions, co-opt their political institutions, and control their productive land."[2] This survival success, according to ethnohistorian Thomas Sheridan, is based on a persistent identity system that is composed of (1) a cohesive sense of collective identity, and (2) the individual relationship with, or participation in, that collective identity.[3] The solidarity of the Yaqui "is reflected clearly in their ritual and religious life. . . .

The Yaqui . . . are reluctant to say much about religion or ritual."[4] Tightly guarded traditions, clothed in centuries of repression and pogroms of ethnocide[5] and genocide,[6] continue to give meaning, vitality, and identity to the Yaqui people.

Our initial project envisioned us describing in some detail the Deer Dance and the religious ceremonies of the Guadalupe Yaqui community outside Phoenix, Arizona. But when the Yaqui leadership invited us to their Our Lady of Guadalupe celebration and an Easter celebration, they requested two things of us: (1) that we enter as fully as we could into their celebrations, and (2) that we not write about them. It slowly unfolded for us, then, that the very beautiful events we had witnessed, and participated in as best we could, were essentially the fruits of centuries of complex interfamilial structures. The whole ceremonial cycle was based on discrete elements that were the properties[7] of certain alliances. The power of keeping those intact, and separate, relied on "secrets," secrets that survived centuries of abuse, ethnocide, slavery, and displacement, and maintained a constant identity as "Yaqui."

This chapter will continue our investigation of cultural memory as a means of resistance based on a faith response to colonialism. Since we do maintain that spirituality forms the very grounding for cultural meaning, our work here centers on the ritual performances that reveal deeply held convictions. Moreover, the complexity of the structures that exist today must be firmly grasped as the product of a historical encounter. For the Yaqui, the fateful point in history that has become their horizon for memory is concretized in the missionary activity of the Jesuits four hundred years ago. Therefore, this chapter begins with a historical overview of sixteenth-century Jesuit activities and proceeds through the Jesuits' historical encounter—and the consequences of that encounter—with the Yaqui.

The purpose of this chapter is not to divulge the secrets of the Yaqui rituals, nor is it to contextualize and explain Yaqui ideology in such a manner that Western empiricism can claim knowledge or ownership of it as another scientific "trophy." We insist that the sense of a people's sacredness is a precious trust that ought not to be placed into a science-biased milieu. We approach the rituals, ceremonies, and religion of the Yaqui people with respect and awe, and we acknowledge that their mysteries must remain the sole property of their own worldview. Rather, the purpose of this chapter is to connect the concept of cultural memory to the structures of secrecy and ceremony as they (1) form the ideology of the Yaqui worldview, and (2) contextualize the identity and the resistance to assimilation of the contemporary residents of Guadalupe village.

McGuire quite astutely observes that "Yaqui rituals are expressly de-signed to attract an audience . . . and even when neighbors have no desire to attend . . . they cannot avoid them. . . . These performances do tell the audience how to act and how not to. And there are sanctions for those who transgress the accepted limits of behavior during rituals and during ceremonial seasons."[8] As outsiders, we experienced a spirituality that has a public aspect, but whose basis is shrouded in a veil that must remain impervious to non-Yaqui curiosity. So while broad strokes can be given here, the real focus of our work on this element of cultural memory rests on examination of Yaqui history and of the continuation of the cycle of being Yaqui that remains today. And that cycle rests in a profound man-ner on the power of secrecy to maintain ethnic boundaries.

Our world is one that is firmly rooted in a cosmology that assumes a democracy and a public forum, in other words, a sharing of knowledge. This creates a worldview that knowledge is public, that it is a commod-ity to be brokered, bought, or acquired as something everyone (theoreti-cally) has an equal opportunity to grasp. Our attempt to delve into the construction of a cosmology that is both resistant to change yet capable of co-existing in a Westernized cosmology leads us first to make appar-ent our own cosmological constructions and assumptions, which flow from a historical foundation based on expansionism and control. Our cosmology differs substantially from the Yaqui cosmology, which is best revealed through dramatic rites that maintain autonomy and community cohesiveness. A historical perspective on the Yaqui people and their en-counter with the Jesuits in the sixteenth century is vital to understanding this point.

Jesuits

The contemporary coalescence of the pre-Columbian worldview with that of the European Jesuits of the sixteenth century is an important ele-ment of Yaqui cosmology to understand. The Jesuits were a fairly new re-ligious order in the sixteenth century, formed as a response to Protestant reformations. The thrust of the founder, Ignatius of Loyola, was to form a group of highly mobile, disciplined, and well-educated priests (and broth-ers) who could revive a faltering postmedieval Catholic Church. Each Je-suit underwent extensive and special training to become a priest and to be missioned to a work of the Society of Jesus (Jesuits).

I will ask Our Lord that I be able to hear his call . . . in the first part, I put myself into a mythical situation. I imagine a human leader . . .

his address to all people rings out in words like these: "I want to overcome all diseases, all poverty, all ignorance, all oppression and slavery, in short, all the enemies of mankind." . . . Persons of great heart are set on fire with zeal to follow Jesus Christ . . . [and they] will not only offer themselves entirely for such a mission, but will act against anything that would make their response less than total.[9]

This passage was the guiding meditation for Jesuits on any mission. A number of recent studies have sought to understand and to critique the Jesuit-Indian relationships in the Americas, but few have come to grips with the importance of the Jesuits' total commitment to giving one's self, heart and mind, to the people of the world.[10] Most of these studies tend to use materialistic structural models as a basis for all human interactions, thus missing the fervor and the absolute conviction that "Satan" was alive and at war with the "forces of good" in the world that impelled these Jesuits to live such lives on the edge. The conviction that salvation of the soul rested upon knowledge of Jesus in the heart helps us to sense the melding of Indian and Catholic affective knowledge. It was a warrior image that allowed the Indians to forge an alliance with the Jesuit reality of spiritual forces.[11]

The point of this description of Jesuit spirituality is that each Jesuit sent to the Yaqui missions had undergone this formation. Each saw himself as living under the knightly warrior "Standard of Christ," impelled to "fight for the forces of good." People who did not "know God as revealed by Jesus" could not feel God's full goodness or share completely in the happiness of this world.[12] The Jesuits were as convinced of their visions as the Indians were of theirs. They were also certain that their words and actions turned wine and bread into the body and blood of Jesus, that baptism took away the stain of original sin, that they could forgive sins in the name of God, and that the other sacraments that they carried with them held the key to being fully and completely in union with God. Little wonder, then, that they could compete with the overt powers of traditional Yaqui shamans.

The language Ignatius used in his autobiography and in the *Spiritual Exercises* is meant to touch both the heart and the mind. Certainly, if one's heart is closed to this kind of language or untouched by previous exposure to such a style of expression, it may all seem pretty "bizarre," as one of our colleagues once commented. It must be emphasized that religious behavior is a reflection "of human creativity filtered through language and culture (and not in terms of rational functionalism)."[13] The decisive notion that the Jesuits took with them as they spread out of Europe and into the Americas was that the soul and body were interlocked and that it was imperative to transform the economic and social order (of whatever cultures they encountered) in order for spiritual progress to occur. That ideology lies within their language of formation and in their myths of their founder and icon, Ignatius.

There is always the danger of either demonizing or sanctifying the encounters of mission groups with indigenous people. Whole systems of cultural knowledge have been lost because of the pernicious and arrogant ways of many missionary groups. Languages have been lost, customs forgotten, and important healing traditions lost to time. The fact that (1) Yaqui continues to be a primary language among the people in question here; (2) dance and ritual forms that are hundreds of years old continue to be used; (3) Indian and Catholic motifs are fused into a unified ritual pattern; and (4) the people themselves, spread now from southern Mexico to Arizona, continue to identify as one people strongly indicates that an underlying structure exists that does not rely on the presence of *any* Catholic priest or "official clergy" per se. And this, it appears, is firmly based on the original fusion of aboriginal worldviews with presuppression Jesuit sensibilities.

What is germane to the nexus between the Yaqui people and the Jesuit priests of the sixteenth century is the search for a perfect world, a quest that has been described as "the daydream for a better life."[14] Ludo Abicht notes that Ignatius of Loyola, the founder of the Jesuits, took the glorification of a knightly past and created a fundamental renovation of religious life based on Augustine's idea of "the City of God." Augustine, sometimes referred to as the "theologian of the heart," contrasted the ideas of the City of Man, built on love of self to the contempt of God, to those of the City of God, built on the love of God to the contempt of self.[15] Augustine believed that the heart needed to be perfected before it could enter the City of God. The heart is the organ that has the capacity to grasp intelligible light, through which truth is seen. It became the compelling motive for Ignatius and the Jesuits to bring the Light of the World, the Logos of God as known in the incarnation of Jesus, to the City of Man.

Instead of supporting the revolt of poor peasants, Ignatius put his trust and efforts into the long-term, in-depth activity of an elite corps of specially trained militants who possessed the knowledge to translate their mystical commitment into effective action.[16] The fact that these militants had such an impact on the Yaqui people, and were seen by "both friends and foes . . . as they would a shaman, a person with an unusual ability to manipulate spiritual forces,"[17] must be viewed in the context of Ignatius's original ideas. Furthermore, the Jesuits were also impacted by the "increasing secularization that not only broke the medieval hegemony of the Catholic Church, but also had its effects upon that order which was striving foremost for the reunification of Christianity around Christ and His Church."[18] To appreciate the dynamics of the vision and the heart training that the Jesuits brought to the Yaqui, an understanding of Jesuit foundational myths and their manner of training its members is important.[19]

The Jesuit Worldview

Much of what we now assume to be the "proper" manner of observing and commenting on landforms was invented, or culturally constructed, five hundred years ago. When the "New World" was "discovered" by European explorers, they needed to formulate new ways to describe the interaction between environment and cultures. Scientific observers separated the land from the biota (i.e., the vegetation and animals that inhabit the land), and the land and the biota from the people. One person, the Franciscan friar Bernardino de Sahagún (1499?–1590), attempted to unify the sciences as "cultural landscape." His discoveries were suppressed by the Inquisition.[20]

Perhaps the most significant scientist of the age of discovery, the Jesuit José de Acosta (1540–1600), published a compilation of his work, *Historia natural y moral de las Indias,* in 1590. This groundbreaking New World science volume remained in continuous print in twenty-five languages for over two hundred years. In it, Acosta demonstrated that America was integral to the world as a whole. America was formed, Acosta wrote, of the four elements, like the rest of the earth, and the indigenous people were human, with their own place in history.[21]

The basic knowledge of Catholicism delivered to the Yaqui was the result of revolutionary, innovative, and controversial techniques devised by Jesuits. According to Michael V. Angrosino, missionary policy of the Jesuit order had evolved from the notions of "imposition" and "translation" to the concepts of "adaptation" and "accommodation" to the host culture.[22] It was necessary for the Jesuits to learn the language of the people of the various tribes and to interpret European theological concepts using Indian cultural concepts. They adapted Catholic images and rituals to merge with Indian images and rites.[23] The intensive linguistic, ethnographic, and theological work of these sixteenth- to seventeenth-century Jesuits became the basis for the Jesuit missions through the nineteenth century.[24] Edward H. Spicer, for example, notes that there is "little record of breaking up of Yaqui ceremonies [by the Jesuits]. Rather, the tendency was to discuss ceremonies and to suggest Christian interpretations."[25]

Historical Context

In what is now the state of Sonora, Mexico, the group of indigenous people now referred to as the Yaqui lived in over eighty *rancherías* covering over 3,500 miles of land, and supporting over thirty thousand individuals.[26] These horticultural[27] people subsisted in the area for thousands of years. Their cosmology was one of a deeply held animism, that is, a relationship with all elements of the landscape as active moral agents. Much like contemporary horticultural people, their cycle of life depended on both concern for all life and observance of rites that kept the balance between plants, animals, waters, rocks and minerals, and the skies in harmony. They did not focus on controlling the hostility of nature, but rather sought to understand the sacredness of land and its processes, acting as stewards for creation. Their cosmology, in essence, emerged from the world they had created through centuries of cultural adaptations that would ensure each generation's optimal adaptation to the environment.

Yet, their world, too, was being drastically altered by world events. The conquest-invasion by the Spaniards into what is now Mexico had been dramatic. The Aztec Empire to the south crumbled by 1519, as horses and new trade goods overwhelmed thousands of years of relative stability. Perhaps most dramatic for even the most remote tribal people at this time (the sixteenth and seventeenth centuries) was the sudden and seemingly uncontrollable spread of new diseases. According to Daniel Reff, between "1591 and 1638, then, roughly two-thirds of the mission population of Northwest New Spain died; some 200,000 native converts in all."[28] Although the census records from established missions produced these data, the diseases preceded the advances of the missions and any direct Spanish contact. In fact, the first Jesuits in the Yaqui area of Mexico (Andrés Pérez de Ribas and Tomás Basilio) report that they encountered an epidemic of *cocoliztli* (smallpox) that could have killed as many as twenty thousand Yaqui only a few years prior to the arrival of the Spaniards.

According to Edward Spicer,[29] the Yaqui first encountered Spanish slave raiders around 1533.[30] This encounter, as well as many during the next eighty-four years, failed to dominate the Yaqui, who were quite adept at fielding thousands of warriors against repeated Spanish military sorties and repelling the attempted conquests. The first Jesuit to the region, Andrés Pérez de Ribas, whose history of the early missions of New Spain is filled with ethnographic details, wrote: "The Yaquis had little contact with the Mayos, or any other nation, their ferocity making them much feared and isolated."[31] Finally, in 1617, after hearing reports of the Jesuits' new farming techniques, the Yaqui made a bargain: if the Spaniards promised to cease hostilities, they would accept the Jesuits on their land.[32] According to Pérez de Ribas, they were warmly accepted, and soon combined the eighty *rancherías* into eight towns. Thus ensued 120 years of Jesuit presence, and relative peace.

Oh, if only it were that easy! Missions and the change they bring are rarely, if ever, passive negotiations. And certainly, with a group as fiercely independent as the Yaqui, who were noted for their bravery, warrior instincts and cults, and consistent ability to turn back Spanish incursions,[33] no ground was given that did not become fused with links to pre-colonial Yaqui identity. Indeed, these were and are not now a group of soft-spoken, meek people; as Pérez de Ribas points out, he was initially taken aback by their "rudeness in manner, so different from the moderation of other Indian nations." Even their name means, literally, "He Who Talks by Shouting."[34]

Thus, we insist that the consistent evidence for the pride, the organization, and the vastness of the Yaqui identity extends back centuries before contact with Europeans. However, real crises were occurring among the people as the seventeenth century dawned. Besides the ravage of human disease, there was also the pressure of Spanish expansionism, warfare with other tribes, and the need to continue to plant and harvest their crops and remain an organized political body. The *rancherías*, organized under principal caciques, seem to have been experiencing a serious problem with consistent leadership; or, as Reff points out, disease and warfare may have taken out many of the principal chiefs.[35] This left a void in an era of great uncertainties and change. It was into this moment of opportunity that the Jesuits entered in 1617.

The Yaqui were a shaman-centered people who recognized a wide variety of supernatural specialists, including diagnosticians, curers, and dancers.[36] At the heart of keeping the cosmos in balance were what the Spanish termed *hechiceros*, or "medicine men/women."[37] Pérez de Ribas recounts that many of these *hechiceros* were women, and they seemed to have a great deal of power within the group.[38] The Yaqui worldview accepted the role of visionaries and people gifted in spiritual powers. Their acceptance of the Jesuits, who specialized in religion and spirituality, may be traced to the Yaqui expectations of shaman consciousness. The fact that the Jesuits did not marry, wore distinctive black robes and crosses, and carried no weapons made them different from the other Spaniards. Evidently sensitive to the egalitarian nature of Yaqui society, and displaying high regard for women and children, the Jesuits "offered nearly as many opportunities for women to be active in the new Church organization as for men, and there were important places for children as well as adults."[39] Thus, ceremonial organization became centered in sisterhoods, brotherhoods, special fraternities and sodalities, choirs, and important leadership roles for laypeople.[40]

The Mission to the Yaqui

History of the Triumphs of Our Holy Faith against the Most Barbarous and Fierce People of the New World, by Pérez de Ribas (1644), is regarded as a textbook on the early missions in New Spain. Pérez de Ribas, one of the first Jesuits to work with the tribal people of Sinaloa, spoke a number of Indian languages.[41] A gifted writer, musician, and organizer, he recounted his own deep fears of being killed, and his many "triumphs." He began a process of consolidating the eighty original *rancherías* into eight large pueblos. By 1623, thirty thousand Yaqui had been baptized, and by 1645, Yaqui fiestas and celebrations incorporated organ music as well as choruses, trumpets, violins, oboes, flutes, and dances. He instituted a religious-political order in which Indians took leadership roles, including sacristans and *maestros* (teachers).[42]

Among the Yaqui, this melding of indigenous and Catholic elements is revealed as well in their belief that "the Lord came into Yaqui country long before the Spaniards. . . . He cured people. Because he was so successful in this the people called him Salvador Maestro."[43] It is also interesting that Pérez de Ribas was deeply moved by all the crosses that the people carried when he first came into the country.[44]

This sort of alliance and the accommodation and interpretation of culture were important aspects of Jesuit-Indian relations in their first encounters. Though practiced with varying degrees of success, they did mark a consistent pattern in mission ideology for some time.

The Jesuit-Yaqui alliances that resulted in the eight towns also integrated the Yaqui religious structure into four "cults," or specialized ceremonial activities. According to Spicer, these were connected to tribal territories that were infused with sacred entities from the mythological past.[45] These cults—El Señor (Jesus), the Virgin (Land), the Dead, and Guadalupe (associated with the Coyote Clan)[46]—heightened the "Yaquis' consciousness of being a nation. . . . Together with their strenuous efforts to keep the Spanish out of the mission communities, the missionaries strengthened the Yaqui conviction that they, the Yaquis, held exclusive rights to the land, water, and resources of the Yaqui territory. Sent by the Crown to Hispanicize the Yaquis, the Jesuits taught and encouraged them to defy the secular Spanish authorities instead."[47]

In just over 120 years, the Yaqui enclave flourished and became a defining force in Jesuit missions, arts, and education. The Jesuit schools opened in conjunction with the Yaqui taught the arts and languages, including Latin, and sent those who excelled to colleges in Mexico City.[48] Their emphasis on creativity and a degree of independence was unusual in the hierarchical church.

During the seventeenth and eighteenth centuries, the Jesuits established a series of *reducciones*,[49] devised to accomplish the transformation of the souls of Indians into Christians through programs of social and educational modification. While anti-clerics and Enlightenment thinkers such as Voltaire, Montesquieu, and Chateaubriand praised these works as "triumphs to humanity," "one of the most beautiful works ever accomplished by man," and examples of the compatibility of "religion and humanity,"[50] the power that the Jesuits developed through them was threatening to church and state. When the Bourbons took control of European monarchies, the resistance of the Jesuits to enslavement of Indians became a source of real consternation. Spain demanded their expulsion, and in 1767, the Jesuits of New Spain were ordered to leave. In quick order, the Yaqui experienced incursions of ranchers and miners, and then successive attempts to enslave, expel, annihilate, assimilate, and destroy them as a tribal group, a systematic repression played out over the next three hundred years.[51]

Yaqui Enslavement and Exile

The consistent efforts by the Mexican government to attain Yaqui lands and to incorporate the Yaqui into Mexican culture met resistance at every turn. Steven Lutes glibly writes that the "Yaqui are fiercely autonomous."[52] The Mexican government felt this in the rebellion of 1740, again in the 1824 attempt to survey the land for taxation purposes, and in the Banderas rebellion (1824–1832).[53] Further clashes with Mexico occurred in 1852 and, during the attempt to colonize Yaqui territory, between 1857 and 1876. Using some military methods learned from the brief intervention of the French (1863), the Yaqui mounted another rebellion during that time.

This was met with extreme punishment; many Yaqui were burned alive or forced into labor in mines and on plantations.[54]

The following years, up through 1901, were years of regular conflict and attempts to force the Yaqui to divide communal lands. Some of the great leaders of this time, such as Cajeme and Tetbiate, commanded large rebel forces determined to preserve Yaqui autonomy. The execution of both of these leaders led to further consolidation of Mexican power over the Yaqui. Cycles of persecution and intensification of resistance followed. The governor of the territory in 1906, Rafael Izabel, instituted a reign of terror in which many Yaqui were murdered, and most others were deported to work in terrible conditions in the Yucatán. These slave camps were deplorable, but many Yaqui managed to escape to Arizona and the Sierra Madre Occidental. Still, over half of the Yaqui population was deported and sent to labor camps, effectively breaking the active resistance of the Yaqui people in Mexico. Yet they continued to resist assimilation.

The effectiveness of this group of Indians in maintaining organization and resistance is based on "a political and military organization intertwined with religious societies."[55] This structure, typically centered on the "gobernadores, captains of war, and *temastián* or sacristan,"[56] had its roots in the aforementioned melding of precontact and early Jesuit accommodations, and is firmly planted in the ethnic configuration of the Yaqui. Around 1890, a group of fleeing Yaqui entered the area referred to as the Western Canal, near present-day Phoenix, to escape the hostilities of the Mexican government. A Franciscan priest, Fr. Lucius, helped the group negotiate for forty acres (La Cuarenta), which is the present-day village of Guadalupe. It is noted in the Guadalupe history that the leading Yaqui positions at that time were those of the Maestro and the Captain of the Caballeros.[57] This village is where we came to visit, to observe, and to be a part of the Yaqui life as it is lived today.

Guadalupe, Arizona, in the Twenty-first Century

At the beginning of the twenty-first century, English is the official language of Arizona. Newspapers recount the modern-day vigilantes that patrol the Mexican border there, attempting to keep "aliens" out of the land. In Phoenix, Hum-vees, Jaguars, Porsches, and BMWs fill the streets; the city abounds with tourists, with wealth, with every contrivance of postindustrial society, and with capital opulence. Yet, just on the outskirts of the city, not far from the university, is the village of Guadalupe. Turning off the interstate and onto Priest Drive, one suddenly enters a different, slower, older world, with *tiendas* (small stores), dirt roads, small adobe and wood homes, and chickens and dogs running in the streets. Here, English is not spoken, and all the small streets, all the roads, seem to lead to the dirt and sod plaza; on one side is the old Yaqui temple and next to it, the newer Our Lady of Guadalupe Church.

While this enclave is accessible, with a large "Welcome" signpost on the outskirts, actually entering into the milieu is not so easy. Jeanette Rodríguez, for example, attempted to get permission to do research here for over two years. It was not until Ted Fortier called on a personal friend, Rev. Dave Meyers, the first Jesuit in over two hundred years to come back to work with the Yaqui, that an invitation was extended. As Fr. Meyers explained, the people have been exploited not just by Mexican and American governments, but also by a steady stream of social scientists. They come into the villages, extract their information, and then publish their findings. Moreover, all too often, they reveal secrets, break confidences, and just plain get things wrong. Furthermore, Fr. Meyers insisted that we not use his name as an entry into the community. "Please do not use my name when working with the Yaqui," he wrote to us. "It is not my place to be determining, much less altering, Yaqui sensitivities to the outside world. My place is to follow, not to lead. Please do not take advantage of my thirty years of work here, and my heartfelt convictions." So, yes, come down, we are told, but come down to pray and to participate.

"Come down to pray with us," is the invitation we receive. For people raised in the Western tradition of set prayer times, and certain protocols for leadership, liturgy, and place of worship, this could be an intimidating setup. There is, in the dominant cultures of the West, a very set demarcation between the sacred and the secular, between prayer time and work time. However, as understood by the Yaqui, as we learned, to "come and pray," means to live, walk, talk, and be present to the everyday rhythms of life on the Cuarenta. All of life is cloaked in a conscious attitude of spirituality that flows through the work, the social interactions, the family bonds, the formal and informal moments of worship. Moreover, all of this takes a time from hundreds of years ago and reproduces it in the present.

What we term "secrecy" is fundamental to this coherency and consistency in the reproduction of memory. In Victor Turner's classic text on the interpretation of symbols,[58] using informants, analysis, observation, and other methods, Turner was able to disentangle the webs of meaning and connections of Ndembu rituals. For the generations of other structurally trained social scientists, it seemed as if the most arcane and private areas of any society should be analyzable, and open to interpretations. What occurs in this manner of penetrating the veil of cultural properties is a reduction to elemental forms of knowledge that can then be discussed in learned papers. The left brain, as it were, appropriates images, feelings, experiences of the right brain, and attempts to reproduce these elements in the vernacular of the researcher. However, in the translation, the culturally specific, nuanced, and particular meaning becomes a marketable item. To carry this analogy a bit further, we came to appreciate that there are "words" that we can never know. We could be present at the Yaqui ceremonies, but we could not record or photograph them.

Our first entry into the world of Yaqui memory and continuity was the Feast of Our Lady of Guadalupe (December 12). The leader of Los Miembros de la Virgen continues the role that has been in existence since Pérez de Ribas first entered the Yaqui River area in 1617. He has the role, along with his wife and family, of organizing the fiestas of the Virgin and of continuing the ceremonies. As with all the Yaqui leaders we met, the family language spoken is Yaqui, while in the larger community Spanish is spoken, and, finally, English where they work. These spheres of perception, formulated by the diverse language competencies, keep the people connected to the wider Yaqui community throughout Arizona and the Southwest; enable them to flow in and out of the Mexican communities, a necessary key to their survival over the past hundred years; and allow them to articulate with the dominant culture for wage-paying jobs and for basic services. As is so important with all cultural groups, however, the primacy of the native Yaqui language in the homes ensures that specific knowledge remains the sole realm of that discourse. This in itself maintains a boundary of secrecy from all of those who need translation.

The role of Maestro (teacher) is one that is also ancient for the Yaqui, and it continues to have a great deal of importance. Before the reintroduction of Jesuits, and during the times when the clergy was banned from Mexico, the Maestro led the community's religious rituals and presided over the organization of the various cults. On this celebration of Our Lady of Guadalupe, the Maestro leads the chanting of the Miembros (members). He is joined by the Cantoras, another ancient tradition, this one of women choir members. And, as the chants proceed, we realize that the songs are from the old Roman breviary and are in ancient Latin. As the ceremony continues, we become aware of the sound of dance bells and rattles right outside the temple; there, in the open plaza, Matachín dancers, a society of men and boys who have taken special vows to the Virgin, are dancing the Gloria Patri at the end of each psalm.

This is not a one-hour or a one-day event. The feast is celebrated over four days, including masses in individual homes and the sharing of meals. Even the ancient site of Tepeyac, where the Virgin appeared to Juan Diego outside of Mexico City (in 1519), has been re-created. Here, the people gather to spend the night, to continue to pray, chant, dance, and to await the dawn and greet the Virgin. There are processions on the day of the feast, with honored men and women taking turns carrying the statue of Guadalupe through the town and to people's homes to honor her. Again, there are more masses in individual homes. And again, the Pascolas (old men who imitate animals of the forest), the Matachíns, and the well-known Deer Dancers dance through the night. Visitors come from other Yaqui communities. Thin lines of charcoal are spread on the ground, warming people through the chill winter night. And men in long, dark coats and dark hats stand guard, silently; they are the Coyote Clan, the traditional guardians of the Virgin.

The organization of the celebration and the natural, easy rhythms of the days are striking. With almost military precision, people become part of the ceremony, cook, eat together, celebrate, sing, and dance. In a letter from Fr. Alonso to his mission superior in 1582, he writes, "The Indians have a power to do sacraments that goes beyond the Council of Trent's understanding of the same."[59] What we are experiencing, five hundred years later, is the carrying forth of that sort of sacramental moment; a re-creation of a time in which people are transformed into what they want to be, and, through ritual actions, a community of many individuals reaffirms their common unity and the presence of a spirituality that infuses their values with meaning.

The values revealed by being present at this celebration are remarkable in a number of ways. Kathleen Sands uses the term "mythopoesis" to describe a way of "claiming knowledge and making tolerable the strange and exotic, a way of coping by alleviating culture conflict."[60] For example, although the Virgin of Guadalupe feast is a pan-Mexican feast, and one particular to Mexico in many ways, the Yaqui have resisted and continue to resist Spanish-Mexican hegemony. Thus, by adapting a complex drama-myth so that it both matches and contrasts with that of the oppressor, a transformational "dromena" takes place. The roots of this transformation reside in the historical memory of the Yaqui and bridge the political, religious, and territorial autonomy that is essential to Yaqui identity. The mythic re-creation of the Guadalupe experience, then, provides double meanings; it matches the general Mexican story of Guadalupe, but it is Yaqui in its retelling through the re-creation of the communities' ancient political/religious alliances. As Sheridan insists, "religion and ritual define Yaqui identity."[61]

If, then, the very means of maintaining resistance to assimilation were to be made public, and to become an open book for outsiders, the Yaqui value of autonomy would be eroded. The transgenerational success of the Yaqui at rejecting assimilation and maintaining identity has been deeply rooted in the land and protected by their community. "Their power struggle with dominant societies bent on absorbing them has always centered around the issues of land control and political autonomy . . . even as they became factionalized and dispersed during the course of the nineteenth century, those who continued to call themselves Yaqui never lost sight of this ideal."[62] To us, sitting through the night on the Yaqui Tepeyac or in the temple, or being with the dancers all night long in the plaza, this was so very obvious; the connections to the ancient *rancherías*, the animals of the forests, and the spirits of the ancestors reverberated in the living prayers of the ritualized lives of the Yaqui.

Easter at Guadalupe

For those who research the Southwest, the spectacular Yaqui ceremonies are well-known events. Based on generational organization, secret religious vows, and sodalities, they have remained virtually unchanged for over four hundred years. And, as with the Virgin of Guadalupe rituals, they also express a way for the Yaqui to "de-Mexicanize" themselves while infusing the community with Yaqui identity. Yet, it is a tribute to the persistence of memory, to the depth of the secrets of the Yaqui rituals, and to their importance to Yaqui identity that although no Easter ceremonies took place between 1886 and 1906, these ceremonies were eventually reinstated.[63] Because of the repressions, the diasporas, and the enslavements, the amount of money, time, and organization necessary to produce the constituent ceremonial parts was not available. But finally, in 1906, the various Yaqui towns from Arizona through Mexico began reviving their Easter rituals. As McGuire writes, "Culturally, contemporary Yaquis are adamantly persistent in the complex ceremonial schedule. Voracious as it is of human energy, time, and money, it is still actively carried on."[64] In addition, as quoted previously, even Spicer, the ethnographer most associated with Yaqui studies, has noted, after trying to explain the Yaqui Easter ceremony, that he still lacked understanding: "I do not know how to interpret it."[65]

This Easter ceremony is in no way similar to the passion plays that are so popular in parts of Europe, though it could have some sixteenth-century connections to those forms.[66] Rather, it is part of a yearlong process of organization, meetings, fulfillment of private vows, alliances with other Yaqui villages, and an intensification of worship/prayer in the forty days prior to Passion Week. The Easter season is "a time of consecrated community enterprise . . . [and] continuity with the past in remembrance of the elders who in the very beginning fulfilled the same obligations, at the command of Jesus, in the historic pueblos of the Yaqui River and Sonora."[67] Recall also the mythos of El Maestro Señor, who predated the Jesuit introduction of Jesus, as well as the *jomi muli* (singing tree), which brought baptism before the Spaniards did.[68]

We have been at Guadalupe for Passion Week a number of times. Each year that we experience this ceremony with the Yaqui people, we experience both closeness to our hosts and a very real barrier that keeps us separate. Even Fr. Meyers, who has been initiated as a Matachín dancer, admits that it took over twenty years for him to begin to be incorporated into the community. The roles, the functions, the manner in which the organization takes place are not written down in any books or posted on Web sites. These traditions are passed along orally, through set protocols of family and kin groups, of vowed societies and sodalities, and in the original Yaqui language. And, again, the remarkable complex of rituals and their interweaving through all of Yaqui society sets the Yaqui apart from Mexican, and certainly American, cultures. To Deer Dance and to do the Easter ceremonies is to be Yaqui.

This round of rituals is so important that most of the employers of the Yaqui around Phoenix assume that their Yaqui employees will not be at work for all of Holy Week (the Week from Palm Sunday through Easter Sunday). Those who cannot get leave from their jobs will often just quit. This is a critical time in the Yaqui cosmology and for the fulfillment of vows.[69] In addition, it is important for visitors to adhere to Yaqui protocol when attending these rituals: no photography, no writing of notes on ceremonies, no video recording, and no sound recording. It is expected that everyone who comes ought to enter into the ritual, and not be a mere observer. Moreover, since the belief is that the ritual dynamic is an experienced reality, it is anathema to try to capture it in a particular mode of time, that is, in a snapshot. One must live, breathe, feel, hear, totally experience the flow and ebb of the greeting of Jesus on Palm Sunday, to his capture and torture, his death, and his resurrection. And, just as with other Yaqui dromena, this one is filled with indigenous meanings layered with Christian ones, all of which are uniquely possessed by and meaning-ful to Yaqui identity.

The ceremonial roles for the Easter ceremonies are roughly divided into three major groups:

1. THE FORCES OF DESTRUCTION

a. Fariseos (Pharisees): Carrying red flags, these men and boys represent the Pharisees, the enemies of Jesus.

b. Officers: These men wear hats and carry white wooden swords, and they include flag bearers; Pilatos, representing Pontius Pilate; captains; sergeants; flutists; and drummers.

c. Chapayekas: Common soldiers who wear grotesque, evil masks, representing the evil against Jesus. The men portraying these creatures carry rosaries in their mouths and pray constantly to ward off the evil they portray.

c. Caballeros: Roman cavalrymen who maintain order and follow the orders of the Fariseos until Good Friday.

2. THE FORCES OF GOOD

a. Maestros and Cantoras: Leaders of prayers and songs

b. Altar Women: They decorate the altars and direct the carrying of the various statues.

c. Veronicas: Young women who represent Veronica

d. Banderas: Flag bearers; unmarried young women

e. Angelitos: Young boys and girls, accompanied by godparents, who represent angels

3. THE DANCERS

a. Matachín Dancers: Dancers who have taken a vow to protect Mary, the Mother of God

b. Pascolas: The revered elders (old men)

c. Deer Dancers: The very ancient and traditional dancers of the Yaqui

From Ash Wednesday through Palm Sunday, at least thirty hours a week are devoted to ritual preparations, meditation, and ceremonies. Men and boys often stay in the plaza all weekend, working, meditating, and preparing for Easter. Their families organize meals for them. And, during Holy week, the Yaqui will devote over seventy hours to ceremonies and their related activities. The local parish church of the Yaqui, attended by both Mexicans and Indians, publishes a pamphlet that outlines the ritual times, the general meanings of the ceremonies, and other information. However, this is published in English and is intended to be an aid to the many tourists and visitors who come for the day events. Because of the need for the Yaqui to maintain silence for much of the week, to remain in character, and to perform their sacred duties, there is little communication between the participants and the outsiders.

When we first took part in the Good Friday ritual of the stations of the cross, both our inclusion and our exclusion were jarring. In the searing noontime heat, people gathered to begin the procession through the fourteen stations that depict Jesus's arrest, trial, and death. No hats are allowed, nor are sunglasses, water, or food. And it is a long three-hour rite in which participants spend much of the time kneeling and praying on the hot, dusty roads. It is a somber, serious procession, stopping throughout the village at homes where the stations have been set up for worship. Children, men, and women all take part, and their serious demeanor, focus, and piety is a dramatic contrast to a similar procession we participated in in Mexico City: there, the priest leading the procession preached loudly and passionately at each station, and people talked and reflected to one another while sharing water and food. The Yaqui procession, on the other hand, was, as my colleague put it, "scary and difficult."

The memory of Yaqui suffering is very real, and it is relived in these rituals. We would like so much to penetrate the walls of silence, and to interview these participants in depth. We would like to talk to the Fariseos and the Chapayekas, and even to get one of their incredible masks (which, although they take a year to make, are ultimately burned at the climax of the Easter celebration). The silence is deep, though; we are invited to the meals at night, and we can enter into discussions about the weather and the children. The nighttime camps of the men are off-limits to non-Yaqui. The Deer Dancers are busy, as are the other dancers, twenty-four hours a day for the week.

Occasionally, a young man or a middle-aged man will come up to us, the obvious non-Indians late at night. These particular people want to engage us and tell us what they know. Invariably, however, they admit that they "used to be" dancers, but have not done it for some time. And, the reason, always, is that they cannot quit drinking. One cannot drink or use drugs and be included in the rituals. And, while these men wander on the outskirts of Yaqui reality, over four hundred men dance all night long, all week long, while over five hundred people watch, keep vigil, and huddle in blankets through the chill desert nights.

At the far end of the plaza, the Yaqui temple is alive with activities throughout the day and night. Not only are meals being served to the participants, but statues are also being cleaned and altars prepared for ceremonies. Next to the temple, however, the Catholic church is an enigma. It remains locked up except for scheduled services. One Yaqui tells us that the Catholic church is mainly for the Mexicans in the community. They will attend it, he tells us, but their real place is here, in the plaza, and in their own temple.

At one of the late-night vigils we attended, a Matachín invited us to take part in a dinner he was sponsoring for his fellow dancers and their families. Setting up some small card tables in front of the temple, women spread out fried chicken, potatoes, potato salad, bread, and an ice chest filled with soft drinks. They fed over thirty people, concluding the meal with a Mass. At the Mass, prayers of thanks were given to the sponsor of the dinner and to his wife and family for their generosity, and prayers were given for continued strength for all the dancers. The sponsor's dinner, in fact, represented a tremendous sacrifice, as he had to work extra hours for the money to provide this feast, graciously sharing what he had with his companions. This underscores the ancient indigenous practice of sharing one's wealth with extended families and being generous. In essence, it encapsulated the Yaqui value system: work hard for the community, share what you have, place it all in a context of prayer.

Final Thoughts

We have been privileged to walk and pray with the Yaqui a number of times. But we cannot tell you much else. We have seen the dances. We have seen the preparations for the dances. We have spent many nights in vigil with the people. But we cannot show you these things, either. We have heard the unique sounds of the Yaqui chants, the sweet music of the particular dances, the deep rumble of the water drums, the rattling of the shells. But we cannot record these for you. Even if we could, you could not feel the cold night breezes and the amazing heat from a slim line of charcoal fire in the sand as it rises in the dry desert air. Nor could you feel the effects of fasting for six weeks in preparation for Easter. We cannot, because, unlike the retelling of a great play or the recounting of a novel, it is important to understand the activity of "prayer" as the Yaqui experience it. In fact, if we did describe all of these facets, and explained them in a logical, structural manner, you would miss the very kernel of the experience: the power of cultural secrets to resist assimilation and ethnocide.

For the Yaqui, the fiercely autonomous Indian group of the Yaqui River of Sonora, five hundred years of oppression and genocide cannot be forgotten. It remains in their rituals, in their ceremonies, in the complexity of their cultural memory. The Jesuits came in 1617, hoping to plant wheat, raise cattle and pigs, and transform the Indians into a European model of productivity. They soon found that maize, beans, and squash made a lot more sense in this environment. Their assumptions about how one ought to pray also became transposed. Through accommodation, acceptance, and understanding, the indigenous knowledge of El Maestro Señor; the rhythms of the land, waters, and animals; and the kinship system of the Yaqui themselves became a living prayer.

The manner in which this comes to be enculturated and made conscious is through a persistent pattern of secret initiations and rituals. Secret in the sense that one must speak Yaqui to understand the connections to the original land of Sonora, be part of the extended kinship system that resisted and endured incredible efforts of annihilation, and be committed to performing the obligations of the rituals. What we are invited to in this case is a profound appreciation for a worldview that accommodates and is conversant with the dominant culture(s), but continues to resist assimilation. Moreover, this example is of incredible value to all people in the twenty-first century who are seeking to understand how a community can maintain political and spiritual autonomy in the face of oppressive individualism and capitalism. The Yaqui, in this regard, continue to teach us the wisdom of ethnic knowledge in the preservation of memories that persist in tying the people to the land and its processes. To be Yaqui is to be connected to the sacred *rancherías* of Sonora and to keep the memory of autonomy alive.

4. The Power of Narrative

ARCHBISHOP OSCAR ROMERO
AND THE OPTION FOR THE POOR

A Contemporary Evolving Cultural Memory

ON A COOL SPRING MORNING in March 1980, a priest presided at Mass in the chapel of the Sisters of Providence in San Salvador, El Salvador. It was a simple ceremony, a daily routine, and the beginning of the day for the nuns who administered the hospital on the outskirts of the city. As usual, the doors to the little chapel were open, and the smell of the flowering trees, the sounds of the birds, and streaming sunshine filled the sanctuary. The enclave on the top of this hill was a little oasis in the midst of the brutal civil war that was devastating the country of El Salvador. The Gospel had been proclaimed, and the Eucharist was being prepared. As the priest took the thin and fragile wafer, blessed it, and held it aloft with the words, "Take this, all of you, and eat it; this is my body which will be given up for you," a bullet ripped into his heart, spewing blood and gore across the altar and the floor of the chapel. Archbishop Oscar Arnulfo Romero had been assassinated. Paradoxically, his brutal murder breathed new life into the consciousness of the oppressed of El Salvador.

In the words of the evolving poem called Monsignor Romero, Hacienda de Humanidad (Archbishop Romero, Home of Humanity):

> Be very attentive, people,
> To all that I come to sing to you:
> They killed a great prophet
> That we should not forget.
> He was the man of the people
> That he loved so truly,
> Preaching the Gospel
> So we can be saved.

Today, San Arnulfo Romero,
You were our shepherd; that's why we don't forget you of all people
  of El Salvador.
The ones in the quicksand, they had you because you told the
  truth,
And to be able to quiet you down, they had to kill you.
To the men of our country you gave a vision when they heard your
  homilies and when
you talked about liberation.
Today, San Arnulfo Romero, in this chair, you called to the repres-
  sion against our poor people who
Wanted liberation.
One of the assassins born in this nation, and the worse to assassi-
  nate you,
Roberto d'Abisoro [D'Aubuisson].
Just with one bullet Monsignor Romero fell down, and here ends
  the life of a great prophet. Today, San Arnulfo Romero.

It has been twenty-seven years since the assassination of Romero. The
question that we bring to this chapter is how narrative, story, song, and
poetry become the grounding for cultural change, for stability, and for cultural reformulation and resynthesis of tradition. In this chapter, we look at
the power of narrative, in this case, the narrative of the life and teachings
of Oscar Romero as well as its transmission through at least two generations. The Romero narrative is a crucial and significant element of cultural
memory. How and what is being transmitted will also be explored.

In the 1980s, a cruel civil war took place in El Salvador. In the early
1970s, landlessness, poverty, unemployment, and overpopulation led to
popular demonstrations, civil disobedience, and strikes. In 1972, José Na-
poleón Duarte, a centrist, was elected president. He was immediately ar-
rested and exiled by the military, whose leaders created a military junta.
General Carlos Humberto Romero reinstituted the brutal military re-
gimes of the previous presidents, implementing government-sponsored
death squads to eliminate perceived enemies. Roberto D'Aubuisson, a
1963 graduate of the Captain General Gerardo Barrios Military Academy,
gathered classmates and junior officers, and overthrew General Romero
in a reformist coup d'état. Salvadorans, encouraged by the 1979 revolution in Nicaragua, embarked on an armed insurrection against the continued government repressions and the continued use of death squads.
This effort was galvanized with the assassination of Archbishop Oscar

Romero in March of 1980. Fearing a repeat of the Nicaraguan revolution, the United States pumped five billion dollars into the Salvadoran military between 1980 and 1992. Duarte was brought back in 1984 to make the country look more "democratic," but the military remained in full control.

Despite the massive amounts of U.S. military aid, the civil war remained at a stalemate through the decade of the eighties. In 1989, the Frente Farabundo Martí para la Liberación Nacional (FMLN)[1] launched a massive offensive against military sites, power stations, and other strategic targets. Then, on November 16, the death squads, aligned with the government, murdered six Jesuit priests, their cook, and her daughter at the Universidad de Centro América, a Jesuit-run institution in San Salvador. Even though over 80,000 men, women, and children had either been "disappeared" or had been murdered or imprisoned, this assault on the Jesuits impacted the world in such a way that the government's ability to maintain its offensive against the civilian population was compromised.

The tide of international public opinion turned against the conservative, military-sponsored government, and in 1990 they were forced to enter into negotiations to end the civil war. Peace accords signed in January of 1992 formally ended the war and provided for sweeping reforms of the economy and justice system, land reform, electoral reform, and prosecution of human rights violations. The accords called for United Nations presence in the country to oversee their implementation. The lack of any real reform has been and continues to be a source of frustration. The Peace Accords have only been minimally implemented. Only 35,000 of the 700,000 people eligible to receive land have actually received a small plot. No one has received title to the land. Co-ops and small- and medium-sized farms suffer from severe debt. Rural social oppression continues and is the context out of which the memory of Archbishop Romero emerges.

In the ten years since the Peace Accords were signed, the UN has pulled out, with the bulk of the reforms still unfulfilled. Today there is no international oversight, because without a war, the world has turned its eyes away from El Salvador. In the lives of most Salvadorans, little has changed. The crushing poverty, unemployment, and landlessness remain. Two percent of the population still owns about 60 percent of the land.

Measuring approximately the same area as the state of Massachusetts and hosting a population of 5.5 million, the country of El Salvador is the most densely populated in Central America, with 238 people per square kilometer. With 8,000 homicides and 26,000 violent injuries in 1996, El

Salvador was identified as the most violent nation in Latin America. Both government and freelance death squads continue to function.

This violence is not new, but rather is rooted in a long history of institutional violence ingrained in Salvadoran society since the colonial period. El Salvador's political structure was based on the exclusion of the masses of people that made up the country, and it articulated an ideology that covered up "*la realidad.*" This political structure ignored the extreme poverty and suffering of the majority of its people.

The Formation and Conversion of a Prophet and a Saint

Oscar Romero was born on August 15, 1917, in a poor barrio outside the town of San Miguel. People who knew Romero described him as a pious and shy seminarian, a lover of ideas dedicated to the intellectual life. At the age of fourteen, he entered the minor seminary at San Miguel, and later completed further schooling at the Jesuit seminary in San Salvador.

Once consecrated as a priest, he remained in San Salvador, where he became known for his charitable activities. "He did not speak against the poverty he saw around him. Instead, he remained devoutly pious and 'conservative' in his political views."[2] In 1970, he was named an auxiliary bishop, and on February 22, 1977, Archbishop Romero was installed as bishop of San Salvador. He was deliberately chosen by the Vatican officials because the Salvadoran bishops recommended a candidate who would not stir up trouble or cause controversy. "Government officials, military personnel, and death squad members rejoiced at the selection of Romero for this important position in the Salvadoran political life."[3]

At the same time as Romero began his episcopal leadership, the Salvadoran Jesuits underwent a conversion that led them to publicly side with the poor. They developed a theology grounded in Gospel teachings on justice and liberation, and especially guided by and articulated in (1968 and 1979) documents of the Latin American Bishop's Conference. The orientation of those documents had already affected their ministries and institutions. By 1973, the Jesuits implemented their "preferential option for the poor" by enrolling students from the poorest areas into the Universidad de Centro America (UCA).

Romero criticized the Jesuits for their institutional changes and questioned the "political theology" of some of UCA's Jesuit theologians. While trying to maintain a neutral stance, and to be a "father" to the church, he shied away from being "political." He did not realize that his silence was in fact a bold political endorsement. Throughout his early years as bishop, as in many Latin American countries, Romero, as a member of the church hierarchy, enjoyed privileged friendships with those in power who wielded the sword of injustice.

Reflections and stories circulated about Archbishop Romero's charitable activities, but he was not yet seen as a prophet or a voice of the voiceless. His friendship and dialogue with Father Rutilio Grande, a Jesuit priest, planted the seeds of his later conversion. They became very close, and when Romero was ordained a bishop, he asked Grande to be the master of ceremonies. Father Rutilio pastored in a village called Aguilares, a poor parish on the road going north into Chalatenango. He spoke loudly and publicly against the poverty that his parishioners suffered. Grande organized demonstrations that called for a radical new land reform that would benefit everyone. His prophetic pronouncements achieved national fame. It was Grande who, in continual dialogue with Romero, helped his friend understand the positions he took and why the struggle for justice for the poor was at the heart of the Gospel. Though Romero was slow in grasping this message, he was compelled and moved by Rutilio Grande's integrity.

On the evening of March 12, 1977, only a few weeks after Romero had been installed as archbishop, news came that Rutilio Grande had been shot and killed, along with a young boy and an elderly farmer. As Jesuit theologian Jon Sobrino later wrote about that night, it was as if the scales fell from Romero's eyes. In that moment, biographers say, Romero understood what Grande had stood for, what Grande had spoken against, and what it meant to clearly choose a preferential option for the poor.

Romero presided at the funeral Mass of his longtime friend. The sermon he preached at the cathedral that day stunned the Jesuits and the people of Aguilares. Romero defended the liberating work of Rutilio Grande, his solidarity with the poor, and his pleas for justice. Romero then invoked the spirit of love and pleaded for reconciliation. Over 100,000 people attended that funeral Mass, which constituted a church demonstration unprecedented in Salvadoran history. This is the moment that affirmed the priests and campesinos who had been inspired by Grande's passion for justice. On that day, it is said, many returned to the faith, and the Salvadoran church was born again with Romero's conversion.

Conversion in this sense is a harbinger of great danger. For it is with the conversion of Romero—who had at one time dined with the military, who had warned about the dangers of liberation theology, and who had largely ignored the social structures that caused so much poverty—that real subversion took root. After the funeral Mass, Archbishop Romero dined with the poor, spoke out against institutional violence, and encouraged people to reform their social structures in light of the Gospel. Romero's defense of the dignity of the poor challenged and eventually alienated his previous relationships with the rich and the powerful.

As the nineteenth-century social theorist Max Weber once noted, it is primarily through the charismatic individual that real social transformation takes place. Similarly, the French sociologist Émile Durkheim proposed that cultures are changed through a process referred to as "effervescence," manifested primarily through ritual actions. Romero's charismatic preaching revealed the depths of Jesus's love for the poor. Romero's sermons and his accompaniment of the poor confronted the metanarrative of power previously condoned through oppressive religious ideology. This shift ultimately killed Romero.

It is imperative to understand the historical-cultural context of the emergence of the life and memory of Monsignor Romero. There are two parts to this context: the historical and the theological. The historical, geopolitical situation in which we find the story of Romero is grounded in the faith-centered understanding of salvation history. Thus, the people remember Romero in stories and anecdotes—anecdotes that make reference to the actual historical context. For example, people will say, "At a Mass in which Romero presided, I remember . . . ," or "During one of our co-operative meetings, I remember Monsignor Romero . . ." "The context during this time was very political. Historical reference was politicized into what we call the 'situation.'"[4]

Most often, Salvadorans do not refer to Romero as a prophet, but they in essence say, "God enlightened him to the reality of life." The crucial element in this statement is that Romero is viewed as one who walked with the people, not one who changed the people's direction. In fact, as we will illustrate, the unfolding mythos around Romero is that the illusions of power, wealth, and all of those false trappings that were so much a part of his "reality" became the false idols of his new perspective.

An earlier archbishop of San Salvador, Luis Chávez y González, set in place the potential structures for this transformation during the 1940s. This occurred on the heels of one of the worst repressions in Central American history; the U.S. Marine Corps had been summoned into the country to help quell a campesino uprising and a demand for land from the many indigenous people of El Salvador. In the ensuing carnage, many indigenous people were wiped out, and the forces of power were solidified in their alliance with the powers of the North. The archbishop, noted as a man who was concerned for the poor, began a process of catechetical cooperation after this horror. This turned into what are the now well-known Christian Base Communities. In these, the common people are able to talk about the realities of their lives, the impact of the scriptures on those realities, and the possible ways they have to address the injustices they see. In fact, by the late 1970s and early 1980s, the Christian Base Communities in El Salvador largely met in secret because they were considered underground movements against the government. This placed anyone associated with them in grave danger.

While Romero was friends with Grande, he was, as previously noted, often at odds with the intellectual communities that linked a political element with the Gospels. Yet Romero, a noted scholar, deeply appreciated the exegetical and hermeneutical methods of contemporary biblical studies. His friend's assassination compelled Romero to synthesize Grande's popular activism with the scholarship of the university. What emerged, as illustrated in the following recounting of our visits to El Salvador, was a person who stood with a unique stature at a particular historical juncture. Through the gifts of his own character and the influences of the suffering poor, he became more dangerous than all the armed insurgents combined. In an address given at Louvain, Belgium, in 1980, Romero expressed his reality:

> As in other places in Latin America, after many years and perhaps centuries, the words of Exodus have resounded in our ears: So indeed the cry of the Israelites reached me, and I have truly noted that the Egyptians are oppressing them: (Ex.3:9). By recognizing that these realities exist and then letting their impact reach us, we have been returned to the world of the poor, and have found it to be our rightful place. Far from distancing us from our faith, these harsh realities have moved us to incarnate ourselves in the world of the poor. In this world we have found the real faces of the poor of which Puebla speaks (cfr. 31–39).[5] There we found peasants without land or steady work, without water or electricity in their poor dwellings, without medical assistance when the women give birth, and without schools when the children begin to grow. There we found workers with no labor rights, workers at the mercy of the economy's cold calculations. There we found mothers and wives of the "disappeared" and political prisoners. There we met the people who live in hovels where misery exceeds the imagination, a permanent insult of the nearby mansions.[6]

As Romero continued to walk with the people of the country, he became active in the dissemination of words of hope on the radio. His radio sermons, still widely popular, became a real thorn in the side of the oppressors, who often attempted to shut down the radio station. As he proclaimed to the world in Louvain:

> It is a new phenomenon for the poor to view the Church today as a source of hope and support for liberation. It is a call that comes from the Word of God to the majority poor, a call to awareness of their responsibility to be conscienticized; to organize in a country that legally prohibits this or which makes it impossible to happen. It is also an endorsement, at times critical, of the poor's just causes and rehabilitation. . . . In a word, the Church has not only turned to the poor, but has made the poor the privileged object of her mission. . . . In less than three years, more than fifty priests have been attacked, threatened, or calumniated. If the most visible Church representatives have been treated thus, you can easily surmise what has happened to the simple Christian people, to peasant farmers, to catechists and delegates of the Word, to basic ecclesiastical communities. It is here that the number of threatened, captured, tortured, assassinated reaches hundreds and thousands. It is the poor Christian people who are persecuted the most.[7]

Thus, just six weeks before he was murdered, he voiced a prophetic call to act in solidarity with the poor. The strident voice that echoes through the decades in these passages captured a country's imagination, and its conscience. One simply could not remain neutral in this conflict, for the consequences were dire. Moreover, while a war did rage, Romero was not in any sense a person of violence. His words never advocated hate, or a call to arms. Rather, he promoted a deep spiritual appreciation of the transformative powers of faith-based love.

While the oppressive powers accused him of being a communist, a guerrilla, and a supplier of arms, he responded with a clear, concise, and honest analysis of the structures of oppression that burdened the poor of El Salvador. He proved dangerous to the status quo by indicting the entire system of global oppression:

> Thus, it is not mere routine that once again we denounce the existence of a structure of sin in our country. It is sinful because it produces fruits of sin: the death of Salvadorians—the rapid death of

repression or the slow (but no less real) death of structural oppression. For that reason, we have denounced the idolatry that exists
in our country. Wealth is made a god, private property is absolu-
tized by the capitalistic system, national security is made the high-
est good by the political powers who institutionalize the insecurity
of the individual (Fourth Pastoral Letter, paragraphs 43–48 [Walsh,
Oscar Romero, 179]). . . . The world of the poor teaches us how
Christian love should be. It should certainly seek peace, but unmask
false pacifisms, resignation, and inactivity. . . . The world of the poor
teaches us that the magnanimity of Christian love must respond to
the demand of justice for the majorities and not flee from the honest struggle. The world of the poor teaches us that liberation will
occur not only when the poor become recipients of the government
or Church benefits but when they themselves become authors and
protagonists of their struggle and their liberation, thus unmasking
the ultimate root of false paternalisms—even ecclesial.[8]

No one who knew Romero ever considered him a radical or a tempes-
tuous person. In fact, his bookish, scholarly demeanor and his reserved
conservatism were the elements that elevated him to the position of archbishop. Furthermore, in his three years of ministry as a voice for the poor,
his peacefulness and his need for solitude and prayer stood out more and
more. Reading these lines and the following quote, one may be tempted
to paint a picture of a rakish, almost Castro-type liberator. Nothing could
be further from the truth. His struggles and conflicts with proclaiming
Christ the liberator, and with reconciling his own conservative theology,
were the themes of his constant interior battle, and an armistice would
not come easily. But, as the following passage clearly indicates, he was
totally committed to the truth of liberation and to seeing the fullness of
life in the people's ultimate freedom:

Incarnation in the sociopolitical world is the place to deepen our
faith in God and in His Christ . . . these radical truths of the faith
become truths—radical truths—when the Church inserts herself in
the midst of life and death of the people. It is there that the Church
is presented with . . . the most fundamental option of faith: to be
in favor of life or in favor of death. There is no doubt whatsoever
that here there is no room for neutrality. We are either at the services of life for Salvadorians or we are accomplices in their deaths.
And it is here that we are faced with the most fundamental reality

of the historical mediation of faith, either we believe in a God of life or we serve the idols of death. . . . That is why when the Church inserts herself into the sociopolitical world in order to cooperate in bringing about life for the poor, she is not undertaking a mere subsidiary task or something outside her mission, but is witnessing to her faith in God and is being an instrument of the Spirit, Lord, Giver of Life.[9]

Six weeks after delivering these words, Romero was gunned down while saying Mass.

We began this chapter with the story of his assassination. In the telling of his story, new generations are initiated into a narrative that shapes cultural memory. Remembering is not about the past but brings the hearers into the story so that the story lives anew in the people. And, ultimately, these stories inform people's actions and constitute within them a cultural memory.

Our task now is to examine how this icon of liberation and of hope continues to vivify the reality of El Salvador. For the evolving memory of the words, actions, and example of Oscar Romero continues to sustain the struggle for real structural change and real dignity for the poor, and to confront the new threats of globalization and the idolatry of wealth and greed.

The Evolving Memory

In our research on the evolution of the Romero event, we visited El Salvador a number of times. Each visit involved interaction with communities of faith in the urban areas, with cooperatives in the rural areas, with leaders, and with base communities. One of the remarkable things that we experienced in this process was the strength of the words of Romero, and in the telling of them through reenactments, dances, songs, poetry, and rituals, they have actually grown more influential over the past few years. The intensifying presence of Romero's persona and the words of his homilies may be explained by the current perceived threat of the Central American Free Trade Agreement and the assumed reinvolvement of the U.S. military in order to guarantee the security of investment. However, as the following narratives and descriptions illustrate, the core of this phenomenon seems to be the manner in which the spirituality of the Gospels are entwined with an active reflection of the realities of the poor and the oppressed. This is a living testimony to the memory of a choice for life afforded by the recalled communal memory of Romero.

El Salvador and Romero: The Cooperatives

In 1998, we visited El Salvador not only to observe the way the memory of Romero was being transmitted, but to witness the memorial to the Jesuit martyrs. One of our first interviews was with a young man who had been active in the resistance during the civil war and had lived for some time in exile in the United States. Juan Carlos maintained connections with many of the networks of alliances forged during the war, and he is viewed as an important leader in the sustainable agriculture movement. This movement is an attempt by the farming communities to resist the trend toward highly mechanized, fossil-fuel-dependent agribusinesses, and to keep indigenous knowledge about ecology in place. His formation as a leader in the community is directly attributable to the influence of Romero.

According to Juan Carlos, his initial formation as a leader began in the base communities, which he joined when he was nine. By the age of twelve, he had taken a personal vow of celibacy and had begun living with the guerrillas. He acknowledged that he wanted to learn to read and write, and that considering the lack of schools and other opportunities, he left the base community as his best option to learn these skills. But he had learned basic educational concepts by being in the community and by being with the guerrillas.

Juan Carlos recalled the impact made by the many priests who joined the guerrillas, and he helped to organize their efforts. In particular, he remembered Fr. Esteban Velázquez, who fostered a strong sense of unity among the rebels. Using liturgies, educational programs, and sister-community programs, this priest brought solidarity to many rebel bands that had been missing. For Juan Carlos, the most important impact this priest had on him was his insistence on the pastoral care of the land, which reflected Romero's support for the redistribution of land, the promotion of farmers, the development of cooperatives, and the restoration of the sacredness of the land.

During the onslaught of the war, Juan Carlos noted that the radio sermons of Romero kept the people's hope alive. Romero's constant denouncement of repressive violence and his call for an end to the oppression of the poor wielded a unique authority. Romero "helped eliminate the power of fear," Juan Carlos said. "We had been living in panic and fear for all of our lives. His words, and his holiness, gave us real hope." Rather than extinguishing that hope and feeling of empowerment, Romero's death "renewed our determination. Even with the importation of right-wing Christian evangelicals from the North, who hoped to undermine our resolve, a strengthened solidarity occurred on the level of the base communities."

After the Peace Accords were signed, Juan Carlos returned from his exile and became involved in the land reform movement. His passion for sustainable agriculture and cooperatives is palpable. In his opinion, the ideals of Mesoamerican cooperatives are steeped in indigenous spirituality, which has been mostly suppressed by the colonizers. Throughout Mesoamerica, however, the indigenous people have been the most faithful to the Romero model of being a church in the sense of "ecclesia"—a community working together for sustainable peace and justice. When we spoke to Juan Carlos, he noted that there were about fifty cooperatives in El Salvador. Ongoing problems with the model, he noted, included the lack of real land distribution, the resistance of the government to the cooperative concept, and the growing demands of foreign investors for prime land. When we parted in 1998, Juan Carlos was on his way to an interregional meeting of campesino farmers from El Salvador, Honduras, and Nicaragua.

In 2005, we visited two cooperatives, Jícaro and San Sebastián, communities in a region close to San Salvador. This region alone boasts over eighty cooperatives, all started in the 1980s and affiliated with the Romero experience. They are composed of people forced out of their zones during the war, and of people who lost many family members during the war.

While the Romero tapes and remembrances (oral tradition) largely recount his constant call for justice for the poor, an important addendum added by the people is the particular recognition of rights for women. In the cooperative of Jícaro, this evolving women's consciousness was especially notable. This cooperative, like others, has developed progressive gender rights policies to ensure the rights of all people in the community. As is often the case in Latin American cultures, machismo often overrides basic women's rights concerns. In the Jícaro cooperative, however, women formed a unit to develop their own store, bakery, and corn mill. Many mentioned that they needed to find some way to generate their own income, as many of the men would drink their money away and leave little for the children. They have also developed a self-run educational program to learn basic reading, writing, and mathematical skills. And, what was their inspiration and help? One after another used phrases like "Monsignor Romero once said . . ." or "It is through

God's help. . . ." Again, we experience the feeling of an uninterrupted presence.

Although Jícaro does have a high production of fish and shrimp from their ponds, as well as an adequate harvest of sugar and corn, they do remain poor. Their organization ensures that they can take care of one another, that their children go to school, and that their hopes for accessible water and land stability may come true. The oppressive poverty that Romero spoke out against so often continues to haunt the people, driven by a lack of consistent medical care, a dearth of housing, and the constant struggle to make payments on land that ought to be redistributed according to the Peace Accords. However, what is present in this cooperative is a sense of peace, hope, and relative safety.

The cooperative of San Sebastián, in the Chalchuapa zone, is at the end of a long, dusty, rough road. Here, the aftereffects of the war are still being felt in ways that are often seen throughout the poorer regions. Many in the ruling FMLN government consider the town to have supported the right-wing government during the conflict. As a result, the people of San Sebastián report that they are ignored and do not a get a fair share of the regional monies. For example, when they requested money for the health clinic to be painted, they received only one gallon of paint.

A lively and intelligent young woman, Melinda Cuellar, leads the citizen's council of this cooperative. She, along with the secretary, the treasurer, and a member of the cooperative, led us through its history and their plans for development. In 1932, Fidel (the treasurer) told us, there were thirty-five families in this area, living in houses made of dried grass. At that time, five of the fourteen ruling families of El Salvador controlled the land, and the people worked to grow corn, beans, and sweet sorghum. In 1963, when Fidel came to this area, people still lived in that manner. In addition, during the war, ARENA soldiers came into the village to recruit men to be in the National Guard and to "protect" the area against the rebels. Finally, in 1991, people who had been displaced by the war began filtering back into the region, and they formed a larger legal entity known as ADESCO (Asociación Desarrollo Comunitario; Community Development Association), from which the cooperatives could petition funds to develop their projects. In a short period, they built a road, undertook a latrine project, and established a school and a little park.

Even though this cooperative is relatively distant from the political and religious center of San Salvador, Romero's ideals inspired the people who built it. Thus, there is a marked isolation from the narratives and personal accounts of people who had met with Monsignor Romero. The people who were in San Sebastián during the war recall listening to Romero's radio messages, and they agree that he was killed because of his stand for justice for the poor. The poverty is stark here. This village has many single mothers whose husbands have left to look for work elsewhere. Homes often lack electricity, and the elderly often live alone. Have things changed much for them? The refrain, heard again and again, is simply, "We live according to the will of God." The sense is that Romero has died, and there is no one to speak for them anymore.

Juan Carlos pointed out that the cooperative movement is a revitalization of the traditional forms found in the indigenous cultures of El Salvador. Based on mutuality, sharing, and communal land use, the sustainable nature of these units confronts the very capitalism and privatization that Romero preached against. The structures that allowed people to buy land as a group, however, also now mitigate their sustained ability to maintain these forms of subsistence. That is, the amount of interest that the banks are now demanding on the loans makes it paramount that the cooperatives generate revenue that can be used to pay down the principal as well as the interest. This forces more and more working men to leave the country to seek wage-paying employment abroad. The poverty of the women and children, the elderly and the ill, then, continues to drain the resources of the cooperatives. The possibility of more competition, arising from the opening of free trade and the importation of more foreign goods, threatens the cooperative movement.

In this case, the memory of Romero is a two-edged sword. On the one edge, the blade is still sharp with the ideals of a cooperative that sustains life, reveres the earth, and works in harmony for justice. It is a radical alternative to the greed, individualism, and lack of respect for the ecology that is associated with colonial-type rule. On the other edge, however, the memory of the power of Romero's impact on indigenous ideals warns those who see the development and control of agribusiness as the future of El Salvador. These developers undermine the basic structure of the cooperative, and so discourage the members of the cooperatives that they have no recourse but to relinquish the land to individual developers.

Equipo Maíz and the Base Communities

Corn is the sustainer of life for the people of Mesoamerica. The elaborate cultures of the Olmec, Toltec, Maya, and all the rest were built upon corn. It continues to symbolize life for the people of Central America, even as it literally sustains life. In his homilies and in his talks on the radio,

Romero often used images of corn and the traditional fare of the people. Romero had a deep appreciation for the ways in which food symbolized community, culture, and companionship. For example, people tell of how he would pass up the special meals prepared for him and stand in line with the people to get *popusas,* the traditional Salvadoran tortillas filled with cheese, beans, or meat. In one of his often-quoted passages, he said that even if they kill him, "his death will be like corn, giving life to many." Equipo Maíz, or "Team Corn," is dedicated to the mission of transmitting the significance of corn.

Organized as a training center for base communities, Equipo Maíz began in the San Salvadoran parish of San Juan in 1970. Today, in addition to leading training programs, Equipo Maíz also publishes a wide array of books, pamphlets, and videos dealing with economics, politics, and the methodology of reflection and consciousness raising. The very core of· the message that the center builds upon is the Romero legacy. According to the directorship team here, the average Salvadoran is steeped in the Romero oral tradition and is conscious that Romero died fighting for the poor. At the same time, there is a competing narrative from the right that aligns Romero with the communists and reinvents him as a person who promoted hatred and violence. What Equipo Maíz must do, they tell us, is to recapture the unity that Romero held up as a value, so they produce photo exhibits and publish his homilies to inspire and give hope to the base communities. Their hope rests in the base communities, since for them, the great concern is that the religious have forgotten their vocation in this regard. It is now up to the laypeople to carry on the Romero legacy.

The methodology of basic reflections, a tradition handed down through the radio sermons of Romero, is inculcated in the literature and tapes that Equipo Maíz disseminates. In this model, the reflections on scripture lead to analysis of social concerns, economic structures, history, gender issues, and ecclesiological conflicts. For example, Romero's vision of a new viewpoint on humanity, based on an incarnational reality of Jesus in history right now, must lead to an eradication of poverty in every sense. Thus, though there is still "much hate and fear," and "more violence, with youth gangs, organized crime, and little hope from the hierarchical church," Romero remains "a very present memory of what ought to be."[10]

In addition, "what ought to be" can be well expressed in the Gang de Los Romeros, whom we met in the Barrio of Santa Lucía in San Salvador. This is a collection of former violent gang members who have banded together to fight the onslaught of drugs, alcohol, and poverty that grips so many young people today. Their residence is amid the maze of buildings that resemble the urban projects of inner cities in the United States: dark, poor, and seething with potential violence. Yet these young men and women have formed Recovery House here, where all are welcome who want to reclaim the memory of Romero and work to reconstruct the ideals he espoused. Each of these young people has a large tattoo of Romero somewhere on their body: on their arms, their chests, and some across their backs. To them, the battle is black and white today: the forces of Romero against the multinationals and the death squads that threaten El Salvador's dignity.

Carlos, the current leader of the "gang" of Los Romeros, describes the liturgy that they hold every Saturday in the middle of the barrio. Usually held without a priest, the services are organized by the people and include music, readings, and a homily. At the center of their devotion, he claims, is the resurrected Christ, who, like Romero, gives hope, "lives in our process, and gives us the strength to move on." The liturgy represents the "way we live," which "is to make a festival of life, to bring all life together. It is to bring the presence of Romero here to the people whom he loved so much. The struggle, as we understand it now, is between neoliberalism and life; Romero deepens our connection to life and to nature."

This is a remarkable example of the seeds of change that Romero began almost thirty years ago. Another "gang" member relates how they need to be with the weak and the poor, as Romero was. They visit jails to form Christian Base Communities there. This particular group of young Romeros see their primary mission as being with the prisoners to give them life and hope, and to help them learn how to build new lives. Again, this community views itself as set apart from the institutional Church, which they claim remains too vertical in its hierarchical model. Since Romero's death, in fact, many of them have concluded that the Church no longer really does much for the poor. The almost evangelical fervor of these young people reminds one of Romero's passion for the poor and the weak. Their insistence on focusing on the economic and political dimensions of the Gospels is firmly rooted in their own personal sense of liberation from drugs and alcohol, and this, they claim, was only achieved through the assistance of Romero's example.

The refrain of how Romero is now outside the official Church and claimed by the popular movement is particularly poignant among the Co-Madres, or the Mothers of the Disappeared. Beginning in 1975, a few mothers joined together to search for their own missing children, victims of the death squads. They soon discovered many other families searching for their missing loved ones and, with the support of Romero, realized how many others shared their grief and determination. Romero gave them a voice and helped them establish an office from which to work. Alicia, a leading spokesperson for the group, recalled how the office was regularly ransacked or bombed, and the very low point when Romero was killed.

This is one of the most moving and engaging areas of the Romero experience. With equanimity and great pain, the Mothers spoke of the discovery of their tortured and murdered children, the rapes of their daughters or of themselves, and the still ongoing search for so many that were taken and never seen again. They recount the killing of orphans by the National Guard, and the taking of children who are now being found living throughout the world. Now, the Madres insisted, is the time of historical memory: Rescue the names to be remembered forever and put an end to the impunity that allowed the assassins of Romero, other priests and nuns, church workers, and so many others to receive amnesty from prosecution.

The living memory that these women carry is fed by "speaking to Romero and our dead children, knowing that we are not alone. We are motivated," they say, "by knowing that they will not be forgotten. If not us, who would continue? Perhaps the Church no longer walks with us, but Romero does, through the people." In that light, each one of the Mothers relates her own confidence in justice and emphasizes the need to continue this work that is so inspired by the witness of Romero. Echoing the example of Romero, Alicia said, "We do not want revenge. We want an end to impunity."

These two examples of communities of resistance—the Gang of Los Romeros of Santa Lucía and the women of the Co-Madres—are grounded in the memory of Romero. Yet they appear to be separate from the institutional Church experience that made Romero's voice particularly powerful, influential, and eventually dangerous. The kernel of hope that springs from both of these latter groups, however, is certainly a result of the base community experience, where their struggle is immersed in the shared values and memories of Romero, which the base communities pass on. It would be a true disservice to the complexity of the evolution of memory to discount the Church from a role in this process. Therefore, we turn to two barrio parishes, St. Francis of Assisi and Madre de los Pobres.

The parish of St. Francis of Assisi is a large, well-organized community in the center of San Salvador. According to their formation team, the inspiration and the key to the outreach to the youth are literally written on the walls: the names of the 80,000 killed and disappeared from the civil war. There are over 28,000 people within this parish, which has a number of satellite parishes. There is also an impressive organization of base communities, with more than 168 pastoral agents (directors of the base communities) within the parish. Women, as well, have taken important leadership roles, taking charge of baptism preparations and catechesis, and developing focus groups on the dignity of women, gender in the work place, and the role of women's work. Essentially, the pastoral workers of St. Francis of Assisi adhere to what they term "horizontal" evangelization; based on the remembrance of Romero, they also need to walk with and be with the people.

Across the city, in what is considered the poorest and direst of the urban slums, is the parish of Madre de los Pobres. The people of this barrio have built a squatters' village along the railroad tracks. Their dwellings are reminiscent of what Romero decried: hovels in the shadows of the mansions. Few have running water or any kind of plumbing. The streets are narrow, dirty, and dusty, and dogs and chickens scamper about in the alleyway shadows. Thousands live in this area, and many have been here since they were displaced from other areas during the war. Some who have lived here for some time recall the shellings and the raids by the military, which feared that these areas of such abject poverty were the breeding grounds of resistance.

At a typical Sunday Mass in the church, the pews are filled early. One whole wall is covered with giant murals of Romero and the suffering of the war. The memories of the past are everywhere here, interspersed with crucifixes, statues of saints, and candles. Hanging on a battered easel is an aging poster with the faces of the many murdered and disappeared from the parish and surrounding area. These loved ones will never be let go; one gets the feeling that the board elicits hope.

The priest, a Spaniard who has worked for years among the poorest in El Salvador, shares the homily with the people. "Where do you find Romero?" he asks the young people. One young man responds, "We have not seen him, but he is alive, here, among us." Another responds, "After twenty-five years, I may not understand the resurrection of Jesus, but Monsignor Romero has not died, but is resurrected in our people. It is easier to understand the resurrection of Jesus through Romero."

An old woman, slightly stooped but dignified in her shawl, stands and says, "Look at the people here from all over. This is a sign of life from Monsignor Romero, and it gives us courage to go on."

Within the barrio of Madre de los Pobres, the people gather during the week in base communities to pray together and to gain courage from their reflections. According to Segundo Pérez, the director of the team from UCA that works with parishes, the Pobres have done much to organize and to find meaning in their struggles. A school, sponsored by UCA, has been established here for the children, and even some of the older people proudly tell us that they, too, are learning to read and write. For the life of these poor parishes, for Madre de los Pobres and for St. Francis of Assisi, the essential message of the Gospels and of their communal lives has become centered in the small base communities in which they are able to review the realities of the world, reflect on them, and find meaning and explanation—a means to proceed with some kind of action, and within the scriptures. And, again, the model that breathes life into this process is that of Romero's example, walking with them still.

Romero: Expressive Culture and Culture Expressed

We earlier stated that the phenomenon of Romero has transcended time through its inclusion in art, music, poetry, dance, and ritual. This area of cultural studies, referred to as "expressive culture," is an especially powerful form of memory transmission, as it encapsulates the emotional content of the memory being transmitted. The context of this expressive culture is grounded in the theological/historical context of the "reign of God," as understood through Romero's interpretation of God's dignity found in the poor. Through popular art (murals, posters, etc.), songs, novels, theater, photography, folk art, and spontaneous creativity, the Romero memory continues to spawn fresh expressions of life in the Salvadoran imagination.

These grassroots artistic endeavors are an attempt to keep political and theological meanings together. The power of the image, the word, the icon, is evident in the continued banning of the movie *Romero* in El Salvador to this day. It is evident that the marginalized do remember. Despite the lack of a center of coordination for maintaining the message of Romero, it proceeds based on something Romero would endorse: the impossibility of remaining neutral. The message, the means, and the spirit of the art remain subversive and, it would appear, continue to be fed by the power of the narrative of radio.

Radio UCA has been a consistent beacon of information for years. During the war, the radio was considered the "only medium for communicating reality in El Salvador."[11] Romero used it effectively, so much so that repeated attempts were made to sabotage its transmission. During a show called the *Time of Romero,* the recorded homilies of Romero were broadcast, giving hope, insight, and courage to the people. In addition, the program *La Voz con Voz* was especially geared to those "without a voice."

Today, besides programming of music and news, Radio UCA gives "voice" to those who have the possibility of expressing the people's needs and hopes. In particular, Radio UCA broadcasts three types of programs that reflect the spirit of Romero: (1) *Good News of Today,* a Christian program that takes contemporary news stories and discusses them from the point of view of the Gospel. People from all over El Salvador participate live through e-mail, letters, phone calls, and station visits. (2) *Let's Speak Clearly* is a live broadcast that takes the radio out to the people. It goes to the countryside, to work areas, to wherever people are gathered, and lets them have the opportunity to talk about their lives and their concerns. (3) Editorial programs, covering the area of "responsible criticism," give critical readings of daily events, including their impact on poverty, the environment, and other aspects of the lives of the poor.

The impact of the radio on expressive culture keeps the narrative of Romero very much in the forefront of the cultural milieu of El Salvador. The musician Guillermo Cuellar, for example, was deeply moved as a youth by the sermons he heard Romero give on the radio. The oppressiveness of death so nearby during the war years gave rise to his music as a teenager, when he began composing liturgical music. For him and for those who heard the music, it helped transform fear and enabled them to move ahead. Certainly, Cuellar admits, he began writing about oppression and the burdens of the poor. And it was through his youth group's reflections on Romero that he began to write about liberation, using a mix of indigenous, Cuban, and Western popular music to express his lyrics.

Cuellar's music became important for the base communities throughout El Salvador during the war, so much so that many of his community were killed, and he had to flee the country for thirteen years. During that time, he traveled extensively, using his music to enlighten the world about the realities of El Salvador. Cuellar, an earnest, artistic man, has never been able to write a song about Romero; rather, he says, it is impossible to capture his spirit in a single song. However, one song is ready for the occasion of Romero's eventual canonization. One of the lines goes like this: "I will tell you miracles he performed . . . now, I ask you to perform miracles . . . follow the way of Romero."

Twenty-five Years Later:
Theology, Ritual, and Expression

For one week in March 2005, thousands of people from all over the world gathered in San Salvador to mark the twenty-fifth anniversary of Romero's assassination. In the intervening two and a half decades, books, articles, films, music, artwork, and photography exhibits have been created to continue to tell his story and to carry forward the witness of hope. The spirit of the anniversary week took in this wealth of memory, and moved through stages of theological reflection, recollection of the war's toll, dance and song, Mass, rally, and celebration. The essential elements of the narrative of Romero cannot be easily encapsulated, as they have taken on a mythos of their own. As noted above, these remembrances have tenacity and a life that continues to imbue the Salvadoran experience with meaning and purpose.

The initial gathering, appropriately enough, took place at the Jesuit University (Figure 4.1). The featured speakers, Jon Sobrino and Gustavo

FIGURE 4.1. Stations of the cross in the chapel at the Jesuit University in San Salvador that depict the crucified peoples of the civil war

Gutiérrez, well-known liberation theologians, drew so many people that a television monitor had to be set up on the lawn outside the auditorium where they spoke. The multinational crowd included people from India, Asia, Africa, Australia, Europe, and countries throughout the Americas. People representing Judaism, Hinduism, and Buddhism as well as other religions gathered tightly together to hear the opening theological considerations of the memory and legacy of Romero. Here, where nine years after Romero's assassination, a death squad killed six Jesuit professors, their housekeeper, and her daughter, people regathered to listen to the wisdom of Romero's vision.

Gutiérrez, speaking of the legacy of Romero, began by quoting him: "Jesus is the homily of God," and, he added, "Romero is the homily of God in our presence." Building on the memory of Romero, Gutiérrez insisted that Romero rightly pointed out the great evil of poverty: that it represents an essential lack of respect for the individual. Using images from Romero's sermons, he reminded all gathered that the racist mental categories that leave so many people in poverty are based on an idolatry of the marketplace. Romero, he stated, firmly believed that "the shepherd does not seek security until he gives it to his flock."

Sobrino, similarly, used extensive biblical passages to underline the need to take a stance for the poor and for justice. Reminding us of the urgency to remember Romero, he recalled that Romero insisted that some things are just wrong. One cannot be silent and neutral when sinful structures that harm so many people are present.

While these theoretical considerations and reflections on the theology of liberation are essential facets to Romero's legacy, the narrative is most telling in the area of "walking with the people." Certainly missing from the gathering at UCA was the voice of Rutilio Grande, urging Romero to listen to the people and to walk with them. This took place, however, in the following two venues: the Memorial Wall and the crypt at the cathedral.

One of the Co-Madres' major efforts has been to develop a permanent memorial to all the killed and disappeared of the war. A few years ago, this memorial was finally erected at Pablo Neruda Park, along the avenue that leads to the center of the city and the cathedral. Much like the Vietnam Memorial in Washington, D.C., black granite slabs bear the names, by year of disappearance or death, of over 24,000 people. Because positive identity is required to have a name placed on the wall, another 60,000 people who have never been found remain nameless here.[12] Walking through the memorial park, seeing the flowers and cards left there, the people who come daily come to find the name of someone who was taken from them, and this places the memory of Romero's strength and presence close by. In addition, there, under the inscription for 1980, among hundreds of other names, is Oscar Arnulfo Romero—in death, as in life, with the people he loved.

A mile from the memorial is the cathedral, where Romero's remains rest in the basement crypt. Although he was archbishop, Romero insisted that no diocesan monies be used to build up the cathedral in any way. Every resource, he believed, ought to be used for the hungry and to alleviate the suffering of the people. In fact, he moved his residence to the simple accommodations provided by the hospital sisters next to the chapel where he was murdered. His tiny room and sparse wardrobe are very different from the usual trappings of ecclesial power (Figures 4.2 and

FIGURE 4.2. Archbishop Romero's bedroom in San Salvador

FIGURE 4.3. The liturgical robes Romero was wearing when he was assassinated

4.3). These things endeared him to the people and were lived with such authenticity that even now people refer to him as "San Romero," even though he has not officially been canonized.

Recently, the current archbishop poured a great deal of money into refurbishing and decorating the colonial-era cathedral. In the basement, where the former archbishops are buried, a sea of flowers, cards, and remembrances from the thousands who visit here each day blankets the spot where Romero's remains lie. His cause is being prepared for the canonization process, but, as his former secretary relates, this is moot, for, as he reminds the audience gathered to hear him relate Romero's conversion from conservative friend of the military to passionate defender of the poor, "the voice of the people is the voice of God," according to Catholic tradition. In other words, if the people proclaim a person to be a saint, he is, despite the Church's reluctance to confer the title.

However, here in the crypt, hundreds of people gather on this spring evening to dance, to sing, and to recall the words of Romero. "Vive Romero!" rings out time and again from the crowd of young people, Indians from Guatemala, middle-class people, and, of course, his beloved poor. Youth groups from throughout the country perform special dances called "Romeros" that have been developed and, interspersed among these, people give witness to how Romero has affected their lives. One young man of about twenty-one tells how he heard Romero's words on a radio sermon and realized he could not be quiet in the face of injustice. It is truly a celebration of a life that continues to give joy, meaning, and purpose to the lives of many.

The narratives here are poignant. It is a time for witnesses to talk about Romero and to remind the people of his words, his deeds, and the continued struggle for justice. It is also a narrative of expression, as music, poetry, and dance coalesce to bring the metanarrative of Romero's life, through his death, to the consciousness of all those gathered. "Even though they may kill me," Romero once said, "I will rise again in the Salvadoran people." Here, in this crypt beneath the cathedral, the people seem to dance, sing, and clap Romero back into existence.

For the official Church community, the capstone of the twenty-fifth anniversary celebration was the massive outdoor Mass. It is a long-held doctrine of the official Church that the Eucharistic celebration is both a memorial to the death and life of Jesus and the source of life and hope for the faithful. And though to the outsider it may appear that the focus of the Mass is on a particular priest, who takes bread and wine and offers these elements to the people, the theology of the Eucharist is quite complex. In fact, according to tradition, it is the total congregation together with the priest that transforms the bread and wine into the body and blood of Christ. Moreover, through this transformation, the people also become transformed into the living Body of Christ. This spirituality of the Eucharist was the very essence of Romero's vocation as a priest and as a bishop who walked with the poor. The symbolism of the Mass, then, is a moment of time in which a memory becomes revivified, recalled, and rekindled within the lives of the participants.

The depths of the Romero memory literally leapt out at this twilight Mass attended by thousands from all over the world (Figure 4.4). At its very onset, the presiding archbishop recalled that the Mass was in honor of "Oscar *Reynaldo* Romero." The crowd, as if one body, held its breath

FIGURE 4.4. Large image of Archbishop Romero used as the backdrop for the altar at the outdoor Mass celebrated on the twenty-fifth anniversary of his assassination

for a moment. Then, throughout the congregation, people chanted "AR-NULFO!! ARNULFO!! ARNULFO!!" For many standing in the crowd, this mistake seemed to further distance the official Church from the people while enabling them to claim a very personalized memory of Romero. Throughout the rest of the liturgy, the chant "Queremos un obispo que anda con los pobres! Queremos un obispo que anda con los pobres! Queremos un obispo que anda con los pobres!" (We want a bishop who walks with the people!) rang out from the congregation. Later, at the outdoor rally four miles away in front of the cathedral, an elderly woman commented, "We let the Right talk at the Mass. Now, it is time for us to talk!"

For hours, speakers, poets, musicians, and singers entertained the crowd and recalled the life, words, and meaning of Oscar Arnulfo Romero. Long into the night vendors sold *popusas*, sodas, chicken, and tamales, and families danced, lit fireworks, and celebrated his memory in their midst. "The struggle is not over!" all were constantly reminded. "Romero resucito! Vive Romero!" (Romero has risen! Long live Romero!). The enthusiasm, joy, and vibrancy of the crowd boiled into the night and did not wane until the early dawn. It had been twenty-five years since a bullet took the life of the man who recognized the voices of the poor and who saw the world through their eyes. The hope, on this night, was that soon, very soon, some other privileged, powerful vassal of the elite would come and walk with the people once again.

Concluding Remarks

The people understood and embraced the content of Romero's message as Christian, with a preferential option for the poor. Romero's central theme was the reign of God that calls forth a new and just society. He did not preach from a "political" agenda, but rather began with faith and scripture. It is through these lessons of faith and scripture that Romero analyzed historical reality. A central theme of his teaching was drawn from Catholic Social Teaching, which emphasizes the dignity of the human person.

The transmission of the memory of Oscar Romero may not be obvious or overt in many cases. It is processed through narrative, pop art, music, theater, and songs about what he said and did. These experiences that call one to cry, to believe, and to resist tap into the lived reality of the people who have been orphaned . . . lamenting their loss but continuing the journey of life in hope. The people took it upon themselves to appropriate the image of Romero as reflected in grassroots social movements and popular art, even naming youth groups, small Christian Base Communities, centers, and institutions after him. Similarly, although many of the younger people in the rural areas never knew Romero, the images, the sermons that are still aired, and the structures of the cooperatives themselves provide an ongoing dialogue with his memory.

Years ago, the situation in El Salvador and the person of Romero did not allow one to remain neutral. Romero wrestled with the meaning of being human in the midst of a suffering humanity. His commitment to the gospel of love and justice moved people as they walked together. Even those who claimed no belief believed in Romero. One Salvadoran woman reflected, "They killed the best and the most in us when they killed Romero." The power of cultural memory explains why, in 2005, the situation in El Salvador and the person of Romero still do not allow one to remain neutral.

Romero influenced the lives of thousands of people. His life is referred to as a point of reference for behavior and for making sense of the world.

Romero was a conflicted person, certainly, and reflected the conflicts of his time. Yet he remains a "flor de piel" (flower on the skin) for those who loved him and a "flor de piel" (burr in the flesh) for those who hate him. He cannot be ignored in Salvadoran history, past, present, or future.

Interesting statistics support a shift that has taken place in the recalling and transmission of the life and history of Romero. In 1988, only 21.1 percent of Salvadorans responded "yes" to the question of whether Romero should be made a saint. In 1995, the number increased to 49.5 percent. Many of the people we spoke to, however, were adamant that he ought not to be recognized as a saint by the official Church. Why? "Because then they will claim him, and make him inaccessible to us." Other questions asked in a survey conducted by the archdiocese were:

> Should the Church get involved in political conflict? (38 percent said yes)

> Should the Church make an option for the poor? (59.6 percent said yes)

> Should the archbishop denounce injustice? (83 percent said yes)

So, is the church of the poor, the church of the prophets, dying out? "Not among the poor," according to Dean Brackley in an interview with the authors. Romero demonstrated a new way of being church—a church that valiantly interpreted Catholic Social Teachings as part of the lived reality of the people. Brackley, an American Jesuit who has written extensively on the conflicts in El Salvador, often described how Monsignor Romero and Fr. Rutilio Grande demonstrated a new way of being church that gave public voice to the poor. These two prophets, and other men and women of faith living among the people, nurtured and defended the people's right to a public expression of faith.

The only source of truth (during twelve years of civil war) in El Salvador was the prophetic church. It was this church that the people experienced as the only true and authentic church. The fact that so many people now view the hierarchical, official Church as reneging on her mission does not diminish Romero's vision or memory. Rather, the people are even more solidified in the empowerment that Romero imparted to them, and they are willing to take on the role of presider, administrator, teacher, or other leadership positions, as we have seen with the cooperatives, the base communities, the Gang of Los Romeros, the Co-Madres, and the artists. To place this in Romero's perspective:

Where the poor begin to live, where the poor begin to liberate themselves, where men and women are able to sit down around a common table and share, there is God's life. That is why when the Church inserts itself in the sociopolitical world in order to cooperate in order to bring about the emergence of life for the poor, she is not undertaking a mere subsidiary task or something outside of her mission, but is witnessing to her faith in God, and is being the instrument of the Spirit, the Lord, the Giver of Life. . . . To give life to the poor, one must give his own life. . . . Many Salvadorians and many Christians are willing to give up their lives that there may be life for the poor.[13]

Thus, the power of the narrative of the memory of Archbishop Romero firmly grounds a spiritual ideology of resistance. Certainly some of this is rooted in the structures of the Catholic Church. But, on a more profound level, the memory of a person who was converted, and then wielded his power for the good of all, rests as an icon of immense proportions in El Salvador today. The emotionally laden images of murals, songs, poetry, pageants, and all the rest propel this memory into a living, breathing, everyday consciousness that, even twenty-five years after his death, cannot be quieted. It is this sort of historical moment that converts the ennui of oppression into the passion of hope and care for one another that is at the very core of our survival as a human species.

5. The Power of Syncretism/Inculturation

THE TZELTAL MAYA OF CHIAPAS, MEXICO

THIS WAS A VERY DIFFICULT CHAPTER TO WRITE, and it has taken many different directions as we attempted to describe and explain an emerging phenomenon among the Tzeltal Maya of Chiapas, Mexico. We found ourselves limited in the language of the Indian people, making us largely dependent on native speakers who are also adept at Spanish. This restricted much of our ability to see into the nuances of the culture and to fully enter into many of the discussions that are presented here. Nevertheless, this ongoing dilemma of translation of cultural ideals and meanings is the very heart of our work. How does the process of syncretism[1] take place, and how are the concepts of a dominant society inculturated?[2] Central to this discourse is the notion that a people's spirituality forms the very foundation of meaning for their cultural values. How these core values become infused with new connotations, yet resist the hegemony of assimilation, is precisely what animates this chapter.

At a meeting in 2003, the bishop of Chiapas asked some Tzeltal leaders what would happen to them (the Indians) if he and all the Jesuits were killed in a plane crash. After some consultation among themselves, one of the elders responded:

> "Jtatik[3] bishop, we think that perhaps you and the missionaries are not doing your job correctly. You see, we know through scripture that our Lord Jesus Christ formed his followers during three years. Then he was killed on the cross, resurrected, and lived among his disciples for another forty days, at the end of which he left them to go to heaven. But his work is still present among us two thousand years later. However, you have been here for sixteen years, and we still need your presence to continue in our faith life. What did our Lord do that you are not doing now?" Then he ventured the answer: "Before he left, our Lord Jesus Christ left his Holy Spirit to continue his work. But you have not given us this Spirit. You have not shared

it with us Tzeltal. It is true that we receive the Holy Spirit in our baptism, in our confirmation, in other sacraments. But you have not given us the Spirit that builds the community and keeps it united. If you give this Spirit to us, then you will see how your work continues, even if you have to leave us."[4]

The purpose of this chapter is to examine some of the ways in which the process of inculturation is taking place among the Tzeltal people today. We combine historical research, anthropological fieldwork, and theological reflection in order to grasp some of the pertinent concepts that inform this aspect of cultural memory. For, as the Tzeltal negotiate the continuation of their identity as people of the land in Chiapas, they are challenged with the task of reinterpreting ancient forms of wisdom that enabled generations to live, and live well, with the realities of an ever-expanding globalized community.

Our work with the Tzeltal-speaking Maya communities of Chiapas provides an important example of the autonomy, strength, and importance of cultural resistance. Located as it is in the southernmost state of Mexico, bordering Guatemala, this ethnic enclave became a historically marginalized area that, prior to the Spanish Conquest, was an important center of Maya rituals and ceremonies. Usually considered a backwater, a far-off outpost, or a pristine example of colonialism, the state of Chiapas has been a venue of active paramilitary resistance since 1994. It is also the venue of a peaceful, spiritual transformation that seeks to deepen ethnic identity.

The Tzeltal Maya Indians of Mexico

In the first week of February 2003, over five hundred men, women, and children traveled from hundreds of scattered villages to Ch'ich to attend a biannual week of sharing, training, and development of their roles as Tzeltal spiritual leaders. Each had to leave fields, work, elders needing care, and other responsibilities in the hands of others in order to make this trek. The villagers of Ch'ich, a small jungle enclave surrounded by fields of beans, squash, maize, and coffee, organized themselves to feed all their guests, make sure all had a place to sleep, and host the various events for the week. Groups of men and women discussed issues of justice, and how to understand the Tzeltal concept of this term. Others met and discussed the role of healing in the various communities. Still others divided up to talk about leadership and teaching. All came together to reaffirm their identity as Tzeltal Maya Indians, whose thousands of years of existence on this land is once again in peril. The very foundation of cultural identity, as we have maintained in this book, is grounded on a persistent spirituality that informs and feeds all other branches of consciousness. In order to maintain place and identity in the twenty-first century, the Tzeltal Maya are actively negotiating ancient patterns of existence with contemporary interpretations of the dominant Christian religion of Mexico. What is emerging is a syncretic autochthonous community.[5]

We began this book by stating that it was a collaboration between an anthropologist and a theologian, between a cultural anthropologist who has spent many years working with various indigenous groups and a theologian who is well known in the fields of Latin American and liberation theologies. Thus, while Fortier prefers to use the term "syncretism," and Rodríguez, "inculturation," we are specifically examining the same phenomenon: the incorporation of the religion of a dominant culture into that of a colonized culture. And, in the process, social structures and relationships are reinterpreted. The power of memory, in this particular case, illustrates the active dialogue of the traditional social structures of the Tzeltal as they reinterpret and adapt the Christian religion to their own.

Behind this action of incorporating a dominant religion into an indigenous one, however, lies another structural element that has been working to maintain cultural autonomy and survival. This element is the Jesuit mission located in Bachajón. In a manner that has been played out repeatedly among indigenous people, the hierarchical Catholic Church initially imposed a regime of drastic cultural change among the Indians. Catholic missionaries forcefully brought their faith to the Tzeltal people in Chiapas. They believed they were bringing salvation to a pagan people and consequently imposed Western culture and practice, largely ignoring the existing identity of the Maya. The levels of syncretism that have occurred, however, are often surprising for the missionaries and for later ethnographers and other cultural workers. Thus, in the Chiapas region, when the early Dominican friars arrived, those missionaries did find a highly spiritual people, on whom they imposed a system of Western spirituality. The resulting oppression became a source of resistance and of reinterpretation of ancient ways alongside Catholic theological constructs. This was possible because of the relative scarcity of Catholic priests, the far-flung villages, and the relatively large indigenous populations. The winds of change that revolution brought to Mexico, the expulsion of the Catholic Church, the reinterpretation of Vatican II, and the rise of liberation theology set an important stage for the alliances that we are now examining.

We wish to highlight two operative and essential elements in the syncretic process. The first is the indigenous struggle for self-rule and survival. The strength of the people to unite, and to see themselves as an extended community, is an essential part of the Tzeltal worldview, as opposed to Western constructs, in that the community has greater priority than the individual. The second essential component is the focus of the community on the Church as an icon and a center for their communal action. Through the Jesuit missionaries, the Roman Catholic Church embarked on a new path: dialogue with the people, encouraging them to explore their unique cultural forms of religious expression within the Catholic context. This dialogue provided opportunities for the people to learn to integrate their faith into their daily lives, within a particular cultural reality and moment in history. However, although much of the contemporary literature is reflected through the eyes of the Western-educated missionaries, we insist that the activity of negotiation is actually in the hands of the indigenous people.

Certainly, it can be jarring for many to reconcile the colonial history of the Church with the struggle for autonomy that exists today among the Indian people. The significant element here, however, is the active participation by Indian leaders in the formation and direction of each Indian community. Rather than being the passive receptors of Church doctrine, they are the animators of their respective communities. In fact, the term "animador de corazón" (animator of the heart) refers to the role of deacons—and "deacon" is not a term for an individual but for the traditional partnership of a married man and woman who function together as "a deacon." The context for this dynamic is based on the reality and cultural context of the people in Chiapas today.

Historical and Ethnographic Notes

The oppression of poverty, together with the natural richness of the Tzeltal land and the historical trauma caused by colonialism and globalization, sets the stage for a response to the cultural endangerment that is based on human rights ideals. Cultural survival has become a major concern for many different groups, from indigenous organizations to world bodies such as the United Nations, in the past fifty years. This is largely because of a growing consciousness of the need to maintain diversification of human beings on the globe, which will help (1) maintain ecological balances, (2) continue to bring new ways of knowing to the table, and (3) recognize the rights of groups to determine their own destinies. This need for a

FIGURE 5.1. Palenque, a Maya ceremonial center in Chiapas

concerted effort to appreciate the native ways of knowing, learning, caring for one another, and practicing their cultural traditions has resulted in increased understanding of how enculturation took place and was incorporated into the internal organization of the traditional society.

Tzeltal Mayan, part of the Mayan linguistic family, today is spoken by about 375,000 people (making it the fourth-largest language group in Mexico).[6] The Maya, of course, are usually associated with their large ceremonial complexes, such as Palenque (Figure 5.1), Tikal, Copán, or Yaxchilán, located in the region that includes Mexico, Belize, Guatemala, and Honduras; all of these collapsed by the tenth century due to internal conflicts and, possibly, climatic changes. Using glotto-chronological methods for dating languages, it appears that Proto-Tzeltal began developing around the eighth century BCE. This dialectic group settled in the eastern part of the contemporary province of Chiapas around 300–600 BCE, and probably separated from the neighboring Tzotzil dialect around 1200 BCE.[7] Because of the widely scattered communities, and the relative isolation of many groups, the contemporary Tzeltal speak two main dialects, highland (or Oxchuc) and lowland (or Bachajonteco). Each of these two main groups is also divided into subdialects. However, as with most dialectical variations, these reflect geographical peculiarities and are mutually intelligible. Today, there are about 50,000 Tzeltal Indians in the Chiapas region.

The first contact between Spaniards and the people of Chiapas came in 1522, when Hernán Cortés dispatched tax collectors to the area after the northern part of Mexico was subdued. Soon after, in 1523, Luis Marín, one of Cortés's officers, arrived in Chiapas to begin the Spanish Conquest in that area. Although Marín was able to pacify some of the indigenous groups, his forces met with fierce resistance from the Tzotzil Indians in the highlands. After three years of struggle, Marín had still not been able to bring the natives of Chiapas under complete control. To finish the job, the Spaniards dispatched a new military expedition under the command of Diego de Mazariegos. But, faced with capture and slavery, many indigenous warriors preferred death to the loss of their freedom. In the Battle of Tepetchia, many Indians jumped to their deaths in Cañón del Sumidero rather than submit to the foreign invaders.[8]

Indigenous resistance was weakened by continual warfare with the Spaniards as well as disease, and Spanish control was established through most of Chiapas by the end of 1528, with both the Tzotzil and Tzeltal Indians subdued. On March 31, 1528, Captain Mazariegos established the Ciudad Real in the Valley of Jovel. Ciudad Real—which was later renamed San Cristóbal de las Casas—would be the capital of the province for 364 years.[9]

As always, the Spaniards quickly followed the conquest with the establishment of missions. In this case, Pope Paul III established the Diocese of Chiapas in 1538, and in 1541 the first bishop was appointed. However, following the arduous journey to the area, he died and was replaced by the well-known defender of Indian rights, Fray Bartolomé de Las Casas.[10] According to the latter's own directives, the Indians needed active protection from the exploitation of the conquistadors. Laying down important foundations for the missions, he advocated the recognition of the rights and dignity of the Indian population and the need to adapt the preaching of the Gospel to the Indian cultures (and emphasized the learning of the culture and languages). Las Casas called for a conversion that would be based on the Indians' free acceptance, and he ruled out force. Missioners were asked to reach out to the Indians as itinerant pastors, and the Church would defend the cause of Indians denouncing injustices and abuses on the part of the Spanish or Mestizo population.[11]

These directives appear to have been followed initially, but in subsequent years, prior to the expulsion of all priests during the Mexican

Revolution, they became more lax. In fact, the Spanish colonial administration introduced the *encomienda* system[12] into Chiapas, virtually reducing the indigenous population to slavery and bondage. Forced to pay tribute twice a year, the Chiapas natives carried an undercurrent of resentment from one generation to another.

Chiapas is a region that has experienced centuries of conflict between the dominant cultures and the indigenous people. The revolt of the Tzeltal communities in Los Altos in 1712, for example, included their allies, the Tzotzil and the Chol. The ongoing border disputes with Guatemala date back to the time of Mexican independence. Many indigenous people favored their continued unity with Guatemala, but the elites, or landowners, pushed for the incorporation of the state of Chiapas into Mexico. The conflicts over this led to the occupation of Chiapas by the army of Antonio López de Santa Anna (1842), mainly out of fears that a "caste war" would break out against the ruling elites. The area's indigenous people did rise up in a rebellion (1868–1872) in an attempt to regain land taken by elites from the north. Even today, the Mexican army keeps a strong, and visible, presence in much of the state.

The persistent attempts to destroy indigenous culture and to incorporate the people into the great nation-state concept are also revealed in the historical census data. According to the 1814 census, for example, about 105,000 Indians, 21,000 mestizos, and 3,000 Spaniards lived in the state of Chiapas. It is important to note here the very early presence of such significant numbers of non-Indians in the region. These are the groups that claimed large expanses of land, encroaching on communal lands of the Indians. For, by the time of the 1895 federal census, the indigenous population was 129,000 people, accounting for 36 percent of the population. This is notable for at least two reasons: (1) the slight increase in indigenous population indicates a struggle to maintain a viable replacement population to balance the many deaths, and (2) the fact that the Indians had become a minority in the region over such a brief period.

A shift occurs, however, in the early twentieth century and continues to be an important factor in the increasing indigenous resistance to outside encroachment. For example, in the 1921 census, over 47 percent of the population (200,000 people) self-described themselves as "pure Indian." However, of this number, only 27 percent claimed they could speak their indigenous language (of which Tzeltal was the largest component). Yet, by 1990, more than 716,000 people spoke over fifty-one indigenous languages in the region (another 245,000 classified as Indians could not speak their native language). In addition, by 2000, the population of

TABLE 5.1. Indigenous Populations in Chiapas, Mexico, 1992

GROUP	POPULATION	PERCENTAGE OF TOTAL POPULATION OF CHIAPAS
Tzeltal	322,224	9.0
Tzotzil	306,854	8.5
Chol	119,118	3.3
Zoque	87,302	2.4
Tojolabal (Chuj)	66,280	1.8
Mam	23,423	0.6
Mochó	8,184	0.2
Cakchiquel	3,510	0.09
Lacandón	630	0.0008
Other indigenous groups	21,541	0.6
Total	959,066	3,584,786

Source: http://www.travelchiapas.com/about/about-5.php

those people five years old and above who speak their own language rose to over 809,000. Yet, the percentage of Indians to non-Indians continues to fall; out of a total state population of over 3 million people, less than 35 percent are Indian.[13]

Three important observations can be made from these data. The first is that, in spite of constant incursions into their communities and pressures to assimilate, the indigenous populations are growing. Second, the indigenous people are not only resisting linguistic imperialism, but are growing as a population of native-language speakers. However, third, the indigenous people are losing ground to the steady stream of non-Indians coming into their region. The fact that they are a minority within the state of Chiapas, yet maintain boundaries based on linguistic differences, indicates, to us, that a pervasive and deep-seated manner of understanding place and being in their world is dependent on a language that is reflective of their place in nature.[14]

The ethnic distribution of Chiapas is very complex and represents a dynamic, ever-changing phenomenon. Even today, out of Chiapas's 111 municipalities, 99 have significant indigenous populations, the majority of which are closely related Mayan-speaking groups (Table 5.1). In the 2000 census, 13 municipalities of Chiapas contained indigenous populations that made up at least 98 percent of the total population of the *municipio* (municipality). In all, 22 *municipios* had indigenous populations over 90 percent, and 36 *municipios* had native populations exceeding 50 percent. This, of course, clearly indicates that the Indian populations are concentrated in a few areas, which also helps to maintain their sense of identity. (The largest concentration of indigenous-language-speaking individuals is living in five of Chiapas's nine regions: Los Altos, Selva, Norte, Fronteriza, and Sierra. The remaining four regions, Centro, Frailesca, Soconusco, and Costa, have populations that are considered to be dominantly mestizo).

In the case at hand, the fact that so many groups, the Tzeltal in particular, managed to survive has much to do with the pre-Columbian organization of the areas known as *tzumbalil*. *Tzumbalil* means "to be planted" and is similar to a clan system. "To be planted" is a particularly Mesoamerican ideal that refers to their dependence on maize and indicates the close kinship the people have to the land and its processes. One's birthplace is of great importance to identity and to the continuation of relationships with the extended community. A clan system (although these do not occur, per se, among the Tzeltal) is an analogy that indicates, again, how deeply felt this connection is for the people. For, in a clan system, a person is connected to a network of kin-people who can also claim descent from a common ancestor. Similarly, in the *tzumbalil* concept, a person can claim allegiance, fictive (or real) kinship, and alliance to a wide range of others who "have been planted" in that land. These relationships form a basic organizational pattern even today among the 530 Tzeltal communities.[15]

Ecologically, the Tzeltal region is divided into three zones: north, central, and south. Some demographic and cultural variations coordinate with these zones. More fundamentally, however, each Tzeltal community constitutes a distinct social and cultural unit. "Each community has its well-defined lands, its own dialect forms, wearing apparel, kinship system, politico-religious organization, economic resources, crafts, and other cultural features."[16] Traditionally, strong intercommunity solidarity contrasted with the lack of any social or political solidarity at the ethnic-group level. However, as will be illustrated here, the development of the inculturated Church has produced a much-needed coherency as a political/economic entity.

Agriculture is the basic economic activity of the Tzeltal people. Traditional Mesoamerican crops—maize, beans, squash, and chiles—are the most important, but a variety of other crops, including wheat, manioc, sweet potatoes, cotton, chayote, some fruits, other vegetables, and coffee, are cultivated. Regional variations in ecological conditions, such as the relative altitude or availability of water, lead to some differentiation in agriculture. Domestic animals include poultry, pigs, burros, and cattle, but these animals are seldom eaten.[17] Tzeltal villages are noted for craft specialties, and the women proudly display, wear, and sell their beautiful needlework. Surplus produce and craft products are traded throughout the region via a system of regional periodic markets, and these markets link the Tzeltal to the wider Mexican economic system. Finally, many Tzeltal are dependent to some extent on wage labor in order to provision their households. As in the past, much of this wage labor continues to be tied to large landowners. In the first few years of the new millennium, the Tzeltal have begun a system of farming cooperatives, as well as a cooperative aimed at the development of their coffee resources.[18]

All of the Tzeltal communities follow an essentially similar structural pattern, with a town center and a number of communities called *parajes*, which are scattered over the *municipio*. The town is the political, religious, and commercial center of the entire community. The town centers are divided into two sections called barrios, or *capsules* in Tzeltal, each with its own local authorities and its own patron saint (*kallpulteol*, to be discussed below).

Interestingly, a number of traditional forms of kinship organization persist in the face of persistent colonialism. For example, many communities continue a marriage system that anthropologists refer to as the "Omaha" type.[19] In this pattern, land-based horticulturalists pass on land through the patriline. However, patrilineal cross cousins are considered marriageable, as they are not considered blood relatives. This is a reflection of the *tzumbalil* concept mentioned above. In brief, this allows an extended connection to kin in various villages, representing the diverse environmental area, thus enabling access to resources at various times of the year. The underlying concept, of course, is that all related people have social obligations to kin when they are called upon for help or assistance.[20] However, as the Latino concept of bilateral kinship (claiming blood descent from both parents) and the concomitant Catholic idea of marriage to a person at least considered as distant as a "second cousin" becomes more prevalent, the Tzeltal are finding ways to reinterpret and maintain the basic functions of these structures.

One example of the syncretism that is of particular interest to this endeavor of examining the roots of cultural memory is how deeply ingrained the ancient forms of political, economic, and religious consciousness are to every aspect of the contemporary culture. In this case, the

TABLE 5.2. The *cargo* (charge) system

CIVIL	RELIGIOUS
Ancient: Alkal, Cabildo	*Ancient:* Cofradía, Oficial, Martoma, Caporal, Capitán
(Village leadership group)	
	(Brotherhoods and officials of the local deity)
Current: Comisariado; Consejo de Vigilancia; Comités de Agua, de Escuela, de Caminos; Representante de la Organización; Jueces Tzeltales, Musiqueros, Promotores de Justicia y Derechos de Mujeres	*Current:* Catequista, Presidente, Coro, Coordinador, Prediácono, Diácono, Visitador, Arreglador, Animador del Corazón
(Superintendent; Safety Council; Water, School, and Road Commissions; Organizational Representative; Tzeltal Judges; Musicians; Promoters of Justice and Women's Rights)	(Catechists, President, Choir, Coordinator, Deacon in Training, Deacon, Visitor, Arranger, Preacher)

ancient system of *cargos* (charges), in which the community responsibilities were clearly set out, has been translated into a new vernacular. This language retains the old structure, yet reinterprets it to reflect the present-day realities. As can be seen in Table 5.2, the ancient civil and religious offices continue to animate the Tzeltal worldview and form of organization. These roles, duties, and responsibilities were, and continue to be, built on the relationships within particular communities and the relationships between communities based on kinship.

As noted above, the basis for the familial units, *tzumbalil,* continues to be an important reality today for the Tzeltal people. Furthermore, the manner in which the living space is portioned for the extended groups continues to follow the ancient pattern of *kalpulli,* a Nahuatl (Aztec language) term. Essentially, these are organizational units, each with its own deity (*kallpulteol*), who acts as protector and provider for the unit. These deities have largely become inculturated as patron saints.[21] Belonging to a *kalpul* is a "crucial source of personal identity for the people. . . . A sense of security and harmony is experienced . . . under the protection of the patron saint and the ancestors. . . . Through this organization, each member receives what he or she needs (living quarters, land for cultivation, assistance, etc.). Outside the community, the chances for survival

are perceived as minimal.["22] Thus, in spite of centuries of incursions and
programs of assimilation (see Appendixes 1 and 2), the Tzeltal continue
to organize in ancient ways, to find meaning in their connections to the
land and its processes, and to maintain a distinct ethnic identity.

The Making of an Inculturated Resistance

PRECEDENCE   The state of Chiapas has for centuries been under the
colonial-style rule of Mexico, but conditions in the latter part of the twentieth century led to a growing discord among the Indians. Most notable
in this growing unease was the steady erosion of village autonomy, the
extension of globalization, and the continued attempts by the Mexican
school system to reeducate the Indian children away from their culture.
Of course, the uprising of 1994 led, eventually, to the signing of the San
Andrés Accords, or the Law on Indian Rights and Culture, which extended
civil rights to indigenous people (by the Mexican government). This document (see Appendix 3), however, could remain a hollow promise of ideals if not for the very active participation of indigenous leaders and their
allies to ensure that the struggle of the Tzeltal for their land, customs, and
children remains in the forefront of the community's plans.

The now famous 1994 Zapatista uprising (named after the famed Mexican revolutionary Emiliano Zapata) was a significant moment in indigenous rights for this past century. Because of the steady erosion of available medical services, the reeducation of Indian children, and the steady
inroads global capital concerns were making, peasant soldiers united to
take over several regional towns in order to get their concerns voiced on
a larger platform. This, of course, caught the attention of the world and
catapulted their struggle onto the global screen. Today, in contrast to the
highly politicized nature of the Zapatista movement, the Tzeltal spiritual
leaders tell us, "Serving politics and religion is like having two women;
you cannot do justice to both," or, "One ought not to approach problems
with a machete and stones. Dialogue brings us to peace."

STRUCTURAL ELEMENTS   In 1858, many of the clergy left Chiapas (usually attributed to the revolution's impetus to seize Church properties),
which opened up an opportunity for the indigenous people. In effect, it
allowed the people to choose how to organize and what to do about their
own spirituality without the oppression of outside missionaries. This is
noted as a time of great creativity and a return to many indigenous ways.
The oppression by the government and by the landowners continued to

account for a great deal of poverty and marginalization. However, two bishops in the last half of the twentieth century (in particular), Lucio Torreblanca and Samuel Ruiz, took a strong stance in support of the indigenous people. As part of this, they invited Jesuits to come to the diocese to work with the Tzeltal people in 1958.[23] This partnership of indigenous communities with Jesuit missions is a prime example of the sort of solidarities that can produce greater indigenous consciousness and autonomy, for though historically the goal of missions has largely been to impose their own values upon a local community, the thrust of this partnership is quite different. In fact, the directive of the Indians is to own their leadership.

There are five distinct communities that exist within the larger Tzeltal ethnic group, each with individual traditions and histories. These five groups are: San Jerónimo Bachajón, San Sebastián Bachajón, Sitalá, Guaquitepec, and Chilón. Each group is headed by "convokers" called *jTsobao*. As noted above, these communities were autonomous, with little political structure in previous times. We have found that, through their collaboration with the type of organizational and power base that the institutional Church brings, the five groups have been strengthened politically and economically through their rituals, language, and cultural forms of religious and social expression. This process is one of reconstructing the Catholic community that wishes to continue to be Tzeltal, but insists on retaining its particular identity as an Indian people in the twenty-first century. As Fr. Eugenio Maurer points out, the initial endeavor failed to understand the importance of the traditional *trensipaletik*, or "council of elders."[24] What the Jesuits have learned is that they must (1) learn the Tzeltal language, and (2) follow the ethnically specific structures that have been in place for hundreds of years.

The notion of ethnicity and its integral role in the global world system today is a key concept for grasping the role of inculturation and syncretism. Ethnicity is a category of human beings that is created by nation-state systems. In essence, an "ethnic identity" results from categorizing cultural differences that are highlighted by a dominant cultural system. Often, the enclaves of diverse cultures are subsumed and assimilated by the nation-state, and native languages, religions, life-ways, customs, and worldviews are lost forever. In some ways, a nation-state can be viewed as an entity that consumes an inordinate amount of resources, human and other, in order to constantly expand. The inherent instability of these systems, as evidenced by our current global environmental situation, for example, indicates the importance of alternatives. The fact that ethnic enclaves continue to resist nation-states today is an important signal for the survival of all people, reminding us that diverse enclaves of resistance must be made secure and safe. If not, nation-states that tend to assimilate humans, decimate resources, and marginalize the essence of being human will surely imperil all life on our planet. However, these enclaves cannot exist in isolation, either. Rather, creative partnerships with organizations that can bridge the two worldviews are essential for long-term organization and survival.

Perhaps the official "breaking point" of this consciousness in Chiapas arose during the First Indian Congress, held at San Cristóbal de Las Casas (Chiapas) in 1974. Marking the 400th birthday of Bartolomé de Las Casas, as well as the 150th anniversary of Mexican independence, it was the first time that all the Indian communities participated in a pan-Indian congress.[25] According to Alexander P. Zatyrka, this gathering enabled the Indians to realize their common situation of poverty, isolation, and marginalization. Moreover, the bishop (Don Samuel) put into place a structure of collegial decision making, as well as a process for the Indian communities to actively engage in the Church structure within their communities.[26] In collaboration with the Jesuits, the mission at Bachajón became the center for this work.

Formational Pedagogy and Spirituality

This partnership between indigenous communities and the Jesuit mission at Bachajón is a prime example of the kinds of cooperative ventures that can produce greater indigenous consciousness and autonomy. At the heart of Tzeltal cultural continuity are, of course, the structures that foster enculturation. If a culture is to continue to thrive, and to reproduce the elements that are particularly suited to its long-term survival and flourishing, the manner in which knowledge is passed from generation to generation must be adhered to. Thus, the Jesuits realized that the Tzeltal had developed the *jTijwanej* method of pedagogy, which flowed out of and evolved from the traditional *jNopteswanej*, or "instructor," approach.[27] This method placed the catechist as the *jTijaw ta k'op*, "the one who challenges, confronts, questions" the congruency between faith and action.

The evolution into the *jTijwanej* raised the individual role to that of a group process, enabling a more involved participation by the communities. This process follows the stages of problem identity, reflection, and solution that reflect traditional Tzeltal customs and values. According to the catechists and the village participants, this method allows for the balance between leadership and the teaching role of the catechist and the sharing with the whole community. Again, reflecting on the importance of collaboration and harmony within the community, the structure ensures that the community comes to a consensus:

1. Presentation of the theme (*yochibal k'op*, "first word"). The facilitator presents the purpose and reason for the meeting. S/he puts forward a few points to stimulate the discussion.

2. Narration of the text to be studied (*scholel k'op*, "announcing word"). The material could be scripture, a community proposal, or an inquiry of some sort. The narrator facilitates by expressing the ideas in a context that the participants can claim.

3. Reading aloud of the reflection materials (*yilel hun*, "seeing the book"). The collaboration with the mission and others provides reflection materials and adjunct documents to aid in the understanding of the theme.

4. Activation (*stijel k'op*, "animating word"). The facilitator makes participants aware of the elements that they are to reflect on, as well as the intellectual tools they have to complete the task.

5. Conversation (*snopel k'op*, "knowing the word"). Small groups enter into the discussion of the themes. Each group will select a representative to voice their conclusions to the assembly.

6. Gathering the word (*stsobel k'op*). The facilitator encourages the various representatives to share their conclusions.

7. Returning the word (*sutel k'op*). The facilitator summarizes what he/she has heard and seeks clarifications.

8. The reflected word (*te nopbil k'op*, "apprehended word"). The conclusions will be reflected back to the community to ensure that everyone agrees with the summary.[28]

During the *intercambio* (regional meeting) at Ch'ich, we witnessed this process numerous times and were impressed with the level of participation, consensus, and force of direction of the communal discernments. In one instance, for example, the theme was to reflect on the role of women in the community. The passage from Luke on the healing of the woman who bled since birth was read, then the groups went off to reflect on various areas. As is the custom, women met separately from men. After a few hours of dialogue, the groups reconvened in the hermitage to present their conclusions. However, one group of women decided that the best way to illustrate their message was to act it out.

Taking on the roles of Jesus, the woman in need of healing, and the apostles, the women acted out in detail the scripture reading, making it come alive in the Tzeltal context. Afterward, the spokesperson for the group explained, "The bleeding is the poverty, the injustice, the marginalization of women for so long, and the suffering of the people, as well. It is only when we can touch the Lord, and be recognized as who we are, that we can become healed."

In this manner, then, the *jTijwanej* method takes traditional cultural elements and infuses them with contemporary Christian and Catholic/Jesuit means of interpretation. The collaboration of the mission at Bachajón aids in the training, structuring, and implementation of the constituent parts. But, as is clear here, the real process, and the ownership, is firmly in the hands of the Tzeltal Indian community. They form the agenda, and they address the issues and come to their own conclusions. In the end, in the above reflection process, the people concluded that more must be done to protect women, include them in all aspects of community life, ensure their voices are heard, and work toward their recognition as leaders in the various communities.

The Inculturated Community

Perhaps no where else that we have worked have we seen the ideal of *ecclesia* (assembly of citizens, church) so well articulated as it is here, in its ideal state. The concept of an indigenous church is an idea that hinges on the involvement of each member of the community and the commitment to be responsible for the community and to base their lives on the spiritual values that orchestrate all facets of existence. Ritual action is integral to this identity and results in the recognition of leaders within the community. Furthermore, the self-direction of these groups results in regular meetings and education.

The authors met with members of four key ministerial groups. The Tzeltal "judges" were "those whose ministry is to reconcile problems between people." They are trained in the "methods of social analysis for the resolution of conflict" as well as in nonviolent dispute resolution; Mexican constitutional, civil, and criminal law; and international human rights. Fundamental to this training are the Tzeltal elders' traditional methods

of resolving conflict and handing down "restorative justice." This pre-
pares them to mediate both ecclesial and civil conflicts. In addition to
civil judges, who are trained to resolve minor criminal and civil problems
within the community according to the Tzeltal culture, there are ecclesial judges, who receive the same basic training and also learn Catholic
Church canon law and the established ecclesial process for resolving conflict within the hierarchy.

A second ministerial group is the catechists, who are selected by the
community to become coordinators. These catechists (often men) have
demonstrated their leadership qualities and commitment to the community in service, respect, and the capacity to listen more than to speak.

The third significant pastoral ministry is the *poxtaywanej* (health promoters). *Pox* is the Tzeltal word for "alcoholic drink" and for "medicine."
Health promoters receive training in first aid, Western medicine, and traditional healing rituals, and learn how to combine all three. In addition,
they see their role as one of preserving Tzeltal culture.

The fourth group of leaders is the *jMuc'ubtsej* (deacons), which can
be translated from Tzeltal into Spanish as "animadores del corazón," or,
more accurately, "those who make our heart grow larger."

Indigenous Theology: Overview

As noted earlier, the lack of good health care and the historical trauma
of colonialism brought the Indian communities close to destruction. An
important development in the process of creating a native church is the
twining of health and spirituality. Using outside professionals and indigenous healers, a reawakening and reappreciation of the depths of Indian
knowledge, healing, and place in the natural world is taking place. This is
leading to a new interpretation, a new philosophy of being, which can be
called a native theology. This new native theology is a creation of the Indian people, based on their understanding of Judeo-Christian scriptures,
their own traditions, and their active reflection and practice within their
own communities.

A core concept in Tzeltal cosmovision is that of *harmony*, which animates all of their endeavors. According to the Jesuit anthropologist Eugenio Maurer,[29] the very root of happiness for the Tzeltal is (1) harmony
with nature, as "Mother-Earth." It is essential for Indians to find tranquil-
ity and peace in the environment. This, naturally, leads to (2) "harmony
within the individual," or *nakal yo'tan* (having the heart at home). Not
surprisingly, the complete (3) harmony of society rests within the family,
where spouses refer to one another as *snhuhp jti', snhuhp ko'tan* (the match

of my mouth, the match of my heart). In such a society, it is imperative that (4) harmony within a community is maintained, as individual conflicts usually extend to family members, and decisions are made by agreement of the whole community.

This concept of the paramount importance of the community is firmly found in the Tzeltal understanding of the "patron saint," or deity/*kallpulteol*, referred to earlier. This entity is responsible for protection, for sustenance, and for continuing the harmony within the community. The depth of these connections is apparent in the everyday customs of the people. For example, in each hermitage or church, the statues of the saints are considered to have eyes to see and ears to hear;[30] thus, whenever one enters a church, each and every statue is visited, touched, and reverenced. In the same manner, when one enters a house, everyone in the household is greeted with a handshake or a kiss. And younger people bow their heads to receive a blessing from an elder, who gently lays his or her hands on the younger person's head.

Thus, when there is a break in the harmony of the community, the community exposes itself to punishment from the superior beings (*kallpulteol*). Restoration of harmony is primarily recovered through a liturgy of healing and a reconciliation. In the former, someone who has "wisdom of the heart" is called to preside at the healing of an ill person. It is believed that illness comes from a break in harmony, and the recourse is to restore harmony through invocations and "punishments."[31] In the latter, the Tzeltal *jmeltsa'anwane*, meaning "arranger" or "reconciler," is charged with finding reconciliation between two harmed parties.

For example, while we were in Ch'ich, the judges gathered at one point to discuss the case of a young man who had raped a young woman. The judges (judges usually are a man and his wife) spoke separately to each party, trying to understand the details about the offenses. Then they spoke separately to the families of the man and of the young woman. After this, they brought the parties together, and each spoke to the judges without addressing the other party. The process resulted in a dialogue and an acceptance of a penalty for the young man, as well as reconciliation between the two families.

In another example of healing and reconciling the brokenness of community, the deacons gathered to heal the heart of another deacon, who had lost his wife a few months before. As noted above, the completeness of being a human, in the Tzeltal worldview, is to be man and woman (their term for "priest," in fact, translates as "little boy," since a priest is unmarried, and thus not complete). In this healing ritual, referred to as *la animación del corazón*, the importance of individual harmony is addressed.

The deacon was invited to enter a circle of deacons (men and women) and was given a candle to hold.[32] All raised their hands over the kneeling widower and prayed for healing. Then, each person bent over the man and whispered words of strength into his ear. Tears streamed down the man's cheeks, but the ritual was clear; his brokenness was felt within the whole community, and it needed to be placed in harmony. According to Catholic Church law, this man could not remarry and be a deacon. Yet, to be a Tzeltal man, he must be married. The resolution of the discord was not the widower's alone, but the concern of the whole community as it struggled to find balance in a broken world.[33]

Another example of the inculturation of the indigenous theology is the translation of the Bible into Tzeltal. Many well-known Bible groups have endeavored to translate the Bible into every language (e.g., the Summer Institute of Linguistics), but these are largely word-to-word translations from a European text to the indigenous language. In the case of the Tzeltal, however, the active agents in the process were native Tzeltal speakers. Tzeltal leaders Abelino Guzmán and Gilberto Moreno, who are recognized as possessing superior oral skills in both Spanish and Tzeltal, headed the Tzeltal translators. Working with Tzeltal-speaking Jesuit colleagues, these Tzeltal men, and their families, labored to create a Bible that reflected Tzeltal values, but was based on the ancient Judeo-Christian scriptures. To accomplish this, three married couples read the Hebrew scripture interpretations, and three read the Christian interpretations. "Although the women did not know how to read," Fr. Maurer writes, "their husbands read to them the texts. It is interesting to note that because women were not literate and had little experience with the Spanish language, they were often more familiar with the ancient Tzeltal words and therefore provided invaluable insight into how certain ideas would be best translated."[34]

Some examples of these passages, and how they reveal a particular Tzeltal worldview, are useful. A few terms have been left in Spanish (e.g., Dios, "God") because there are no equivalent terms in Tzeltal. However, a word like "apostle" is now the equivalent of "one who serves." For words that do not exist in Tzeltal, neologisms have been created, based on Tzeltal roots; for example, "key" is "instrument to open." A very good example of a uniquely Tzeltal understanding is the translation of "teacher." The Tzeltal term, *j-nohp-tes-wan-ej*, means "he who makes me learn and has the responsibility of making me learn." "Judge" does not mean, "one who passes sentence," but rather "that person who reconciles the parties in conflict." And, a particularly poignant passage, John 15:4 ("Remain in me and I in you"), becomes "May your heart remain as one, united with mine, and I also, unite my heart to remain united with yours."[35]

On July 12, 2005, the translation was presented to the people in a formal ceremony. Fr. Eugenio Maurer wrote the following account:

> The liturgy begins, before the Mayan altar, with prayers of the faithful, in the Tzeltal way. They prayed in each of the four directions of the Mayan altar (about 20 minutes), at each of the four cardinal points, respectively: to the North, from where the fertile rain comes; to the South, where hot weather comes; to the West, where the sun sets, and to the East, where the sun rises.

The *ambo* [where the readings and Gospel are read] has arms that are the leaves that cover the ear of corn, its grains of four different colors that represent the distinct subethnicities of the Tzeltal people. The *bats'il*, or authentic Mayan women-men, were created of diverse varieties [of corn], which a goddess ground and later used to form the bodies of the first humans. Corn is sacred, and for this reason, the book of the Divine Word rests on the corn.

Just as they prayed toward the four cardinal points, the bishop also presented the Divine Word toward each of the four cardinal points to indicate the universality of the message, which finally comes to the Tzeltal People in their *bats'il k'op*, their true language.

At the end of the Mass, each of the four main translators was honored (Fr. Eugenio, Gilberto, Nacho Morales, and Abelino) and asked direct prayers to Papa God about what had come from our heart.[36]

Indigenous Theology: The New Synthesis

Inculturation is the process, ideally, whereby a new cultural creation blooms out of the seeds of the indigenous ways mixed with the ways of the outside religion. As an anthropological concept, this is what is termed "culture change": adaptation and reinterpretation for cultural continuity. The importance of this syncretic blending of indigenous and non-native elements is that it (1) maintains negotiated ethnic boundaries, (2) creates new forms to understand cross-cultural meanings, and (3) infuses the inculturated spirituality with emotionally available meanings that underscore indigenous values.

This new understanding of place and being continues to use the ancient ways of political-social-religious organization, and to reinterpret those

TABLE 5.3. The process of syncretism in Chiapas

How We Do It
   Insertion
   Inculturation
   Interdisciplinary unions

With an Attitude of:
   Respect for and value of cultures

While Promoting:
   Traditional practices
   Indigenous church
   Human rights

Through:
   Courses
   Encounters
   Meetings
   Cases

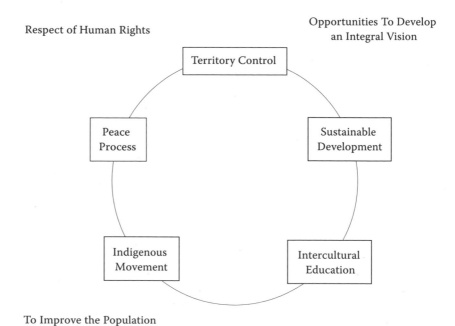

FIGURE 5.2. The goals of syncretism in Chiapas

roles in contemporary areas. So, rather than demeaning and eradicating the ancient ways of sustainability, these partnerships reinterpret and revitalize the rites, myths, and traditions of the ancestors. The Jesuits and the Catholic Church in Chiapas, who actively participate in and serve this collaborative organization, do not set out their own goals to accomplish, but rather articulate the goals and processes of the Indians themselves.

Thus, according to the teams of Tzeltal and Jesuits, the inculturation of the faith is a means of maintaining cultural autonomy and resisting Western expansionism and hegemony. The process and goals of this inculturation are summarized in Table 5.3 and Figure 5.2.

Concluding Remarks

The partnership between the Tzeltal and the Jesuits of Chiapas helps unite the ideals of human rights and the internal strengths of the communities, and underscores the determination of the people to be nonglobalized and ethnically separate from the dominant culture. The Tzeltal people have endured over five hundred years of conquest and marginalization by Western world powers. Political programs to assimilate, to enculturate, and to break apart traditional ways and structures have been actively resisted, as noted in the history and the current events of the area. However, at the dawn of the twenty-first century, new threats take on a particularly pernicious aspect. A few of these, such as the North American Free Trade Agreement (NAFTA), place the Tzeltal people in a new and dangerous position. For, with the opening of the verdant areas of Chiapas to oil exploration, mining, agribusiness, tourism, manufacturing plants, and other aspects of "progress," the village structures and family organizations are placed in real danger. Accompanying these pressures is the steady encroachment of Spanish as a forced language in the schools, as well as English as the language of business. Oftentimes, as well, some Pentecostal sects have taken the position that anything indigenous needs to be converted to Western sensibilities. All of these threats represent forms that lack respect for the culture and the people of the area.

Thus, by developing an inculturated autochthonous community, the Tzeltal gain a stronger structure with which to control their own destiny. With little doubt, the Catholic Church is a powerful ally in their struggle for autonomy and ethnic recognition. By challenging the Church to raise its own level of consciousness regarding the unique cultural and social patterns of their long tradition, the Tzeltal have in fact aided the Church to respond to its own rhetoric of being with the poor and the marginalized and being a Church of service to the poor. With services now exclu-

FIGURE 5.3. Maya and Catholic ritual during an interregional meeting, Ch'ich, Chiapas

sively in the Tzeltal language, meetings and proceedings carried out in the Tzeltal way, and structures of leadership and enculturation placed in a Tzeltal context, the syncretic nature of traditional spirituality and twenty-first-century Catholic theology empowers the Indian people to find the all-important harmony within the land where they live, and in the communities that animate the past, present, and future of the region. To reiterate the basic premise of this book, the very foundation of cultural identity is a persistent spirituality that informs and feeds all other branches of consciousness. The modes of syncretic inculturation that the Tzeltal are developing are clearly based on pre-Columbian structures that help them maintain their balance—and harmony—in the twenty-first century.

6. Final Thoughts

THE CONCEPT OF "CULTURE" is subject to a plethora of definitions, but we have chosen to view culture as ideational. The usual definition is fused with notions of function (how the culture operates to maintain life), history (how the culture understands its place in time), politics (the alliances that bond people to elements of power and governance), and all the other traditional paradigms of the culture concept. By choosing to examine the role of memory in the ideational sense, we have maintained that cultures at their very core are built on an all-pervasive spirituality that provides values with emotionally hued meanings. Thus, by placing spirituality in a privileged position in the formation and maintenance of cultural identity, we have argued that the heart of cultural survival is a dynamic of religious consciousness and resistance to the imposition of colonialism.

In taking this stance, we have examined the roles of image (Guadalupe), secrecy and ritual (Yaqui), narrative (Romero), and syncretic developments (Tzeltal) as means by which specific cultures organize and maintain ethnic boundaries. Theologian Robert Schreiter insightfully sums up this process:

> Culture is ideational—it provides systems of frameworks of meaning which serve both to interpret the world and to provide guidance for living in the world. Culture in this dimension embodies beliefs, values, attitudes, and rules for behavior. Second, culture is performance—rituals that bind a culture's members together to provide them with a participatory way of embodying and enacting their histories and values. Performance also encompasses embodied behaviors. Third, culture is material—the artifacts and symbolizations that become a source for identity: language, food, clothing, music, and the organization of space.[1]

Although we presented four specific manners in which cultures maintain, interpret, and guide themselves in the world while resisting assimilation, all four manners—image, secrecy/ritual, narrative, and syncretic developments—are, of course, present in each example. What is especially important to this point is that our study of cultural memory absolutely precludes any notion of memory being an inheritable collective entity in the biological sense. Since culture is learned behavior, and is intended to lead to an ongoing adaptation to the social and environmental contexts, it necessarily falls or rises on the strength of its enculturation processes. Yes, some postmodern theorists have debated the reality of "culture," but we insist that there is a substance and a truth to the manner in which people construct their realities and organize their values with meaning. *This is the role of cultural memory.*

Allied to our thesis is the work of sociologist Maurice Halbwachs, whose notion of collective memory is rooted in socialization and custom.[2] What we have especially highlighted in this study is that cultural memory is transcendent in that it remains embedded in, yet distinct from, the everyday experience. Cultural memory is anchored and does not change over time.[3] As Assmann argues, there are fateful points in history, the memory of which is maintained through texts, rites, monuments, narratives, and other forms of transmission illustrated by our examples.[4] Throughout, we have reiterated six distinct elements of cultural memory:

1. *Identity.* In a dominant worldview that assumes globalization, the Mexicans, Yaqui, Salvadorans, and Tzeltal stand as examples of the maintenance of ethnic identity. The source of this ability to resist Western global identity is discovered in a consciousness of their unity in differences from the dominant culture.

2. *Reconstruction.* In no manner have we suggested that the above cultures are attempting to preserve the past per se. Rather, the dynamism of culture, and its ability to adapt and to produce generations of descendants, rests in an ability to interpret and reconstruct vital knowledge. How that past is remembered in the present is not an imitation of the "good old days." It is, rather, an activity of making meaning in the world. That reconstruction of the past is never a replicating proposition, but rather a process of contemporary human beings creating a space to exist along with the wisdom of their ancestors.

3. *Enculturation.* The manner in which members of a culture learn core values is key to the survival of the repository of wisdom of

any culture. One must be filled with the worldview that marks a culture's distinctiveness and be so imprinted with that knowledge that it appears absolutely logical. As meaning-seeking creatures, we depend upon our social context to provide answers and guidance. Often, what cannot be grasped on an intellectual level is most deeply appreciated through a process of learning that infuses feelings with meanings. These communally appropriate ways of viewing the world, often inaccessible to outsiders, are the structural elements to the formation of cultural memory.

4. *Transmission.* The structures in which the memory is institutionalized through modes of communication, and the socialization of those responsible for its transmission, are of great importance to how cultural memory is maintained. Therefore, we have examined the role of image, narrative, secrecy and ritual, and syncretism. These form the means for the enculturation of the memories.

5. *Obligations.* The obligations connected to a group's values ensure its continued resiliency in the world today. These moral imperatives, if you will, are directed at the process of developing a fully human being in the ideal of that particular culture. The Yaqui, for example, must keep a discipline of silence, of fasting, of keeping vows, and all the other ancient protectors of their identity. We have pointed out, as well, the obligations of families to pass on the image of Guadalupe to their children and to tell that story. Similarly, those who hear the narratives of Romero are challenged and obligated to walk with him today. And the Tzeltal continue to recognize their obligations to the land from which they were planted, to name but a few examples from our study.

6. *Reflexivity.* Reflexivity is the ability to take the everyday and interpret it in the metamemory context. Thus, cultural memory is the ground from which everyday experiences become meaningful. Furthermore, this reflexivity ensures a "healthy" ethnocentrism regarding a culture's own system of knowledge.[5] We have illustrated how the Tzeltal Maya people, living amidst an encroaching globalized world, use an interpretation of the Judeo-Christian scriptures to guide them through the new social elements being introduced into their world. Perhaps in some large North American city, a young Mexican single mother finds solace and renewed strength in the words of Guadalupe, and recalls the image given to her by her grandmother. We have shown how the Mothers of

the Disappeared in El Salvador find strength in their connection to Romero. And in the Yaqui enclave outside of Phoenix, what appears to the outsider as poverty is alive with the richness of connection to the eight pueblos of Sonora.

Given pervasive globalization and the ravages of colonialism, it is obvious that there are no "pure" cultures. Culture contact, culture change, and adaptations are a given. Environments shift, new information arrives, foreign concepts and material goods constantly cross borders. No culture can remain static and survive over the centuries, successfully reproducing knowledge and humans. Rather, cultures devise strategies to understand the new elements and to connect their core values with the wisdom of the past. The fact that the crucial memories that we have discussed in our four cases are all rooted in violent, disruptive events is absolutely key to understanding cultural integrity and resistance to assimilation.

Again, the strategies that we have described here are the result of active negotiation around the boundaries of participation. The descendants of the Guadalupe experience, for example, remember ancestors who had to choose between annihilation, accommodation, or assimilation. The collective memory of Guadalupe reminds them of the pre-Columbian realities, the destructiveness of the conquest, and the manner in which the ideal life ought to be lived. This is actively negotiated with the realities of the ordinary world, whether it is in Mexico City or Duluth, Minnesota. Similarly, the Yaqui descendants recall the years of subjugation and horrors, placed in the context of secrets that only those who have direct links to that experience can know. Today, the Yaqui on the outskirts of Phoenix, be they social workers or garbage collectors, are joined through a matrix of ritual and ceremonial bonds that transform marginalization into centrality.

What we have presented in the case of Romero and the El Salvador experience is an example of how a destructive event becomes embedded with meaning. Here we have an example of a cultural memory that is being created in an effort to resist the continued efforts to oppress and annihilate the poor. The narrative elevates the horrors of death squads, war, and hatred to a communal obligation to walk with Romero. And in the example of the Tzeltal of Chiapas, we presented the dynamics of a cultural memory that rests on a grounded pre-Columbian past. That memory has encountered the horrors of the conquest and of colonialism, but now negotiates with a former oppressor to bring new meanings to old rituals and relationships.

Our work on these cultural elements of memory is a passion and an inspiration. Both of us have been deeply moved by the stories that we encountered and the people we met. While we each have years of prior experience working with diverse communities, the research goals of this particular project deepened our commitment to understanding and teaching about cultural survival today. For though the globalized, dominant society and so many nation-states continue to marginalize and assimilate the diverse cultures, it is clear that resistance is occurring. Furthermore, in a postindustrial society in which spirituality and religion are either discounted as conveying any real knowledge or miscast as the pawns of political ideologues, we insist that authentic human potential and goodness is rooted in a culture's spirituality. For the many marginalized communities, ethnic enclaves, and struggling communities that are beset by a world that would deny them a place, cultural memories establish place, legitimacy, and voice. We are wise if we visit, listen, and learn.

APPENDIX 1.

Summary of Post-independence Political Movements in Mexico

HISTORICAL PERIODS & DATES	NATIONAL ADMINISTRATION	PUBLIC POLICIES		IMPACTS & INDIGENOUS MOVEMENTS
		Agrarian & Economic	*Cultural & Educational*	
57–1910 characterized Liberal politics and thirty-year dictatorship	Presidencies of Benito Juárez 1880–1910 Presidency and dictatorship of Porfirio Díaz	Privatization of communal lands. Distribution of large blocks of lands to estate owners. Colonization by Italian, Spanish, and French farmers encouraged.	No educational or cultural support to indigenous peoples. First schools for indigenous peoples instituted. Society appropriates symbols from the past.	Beginning of the "caste wars" of indigenous groups. Armed rebellion of the Yaqui, Cora, Huichol, Otomi, and Nahua for land rights.
10–1930 exican evolution ational econstruction	Presidencies of F. I. Madero and V. Carranza. Seven years of civil war. Constitutional Reform/Agrarian Law.	Chaotic division of land in private plots. Expropriation of large holdings and recognize *comunidades*. Create *ejidos*.	Ethnographic studies initiated and solutions proposed. Creation of a Department of Education and Indigenous Boarding Schools.	Zapatista movement for land begins in Morelos. Slogan is "Land and Liberty." Sociedad Unificadora de la Raza Indígena (SURI) created.

HISTORICAL PERIODS & DATES	NATIONAL ADMINISTRATION	PUBLIC POLICIES		IMPACTS & INDIGENOUS MOVEMENTS
		Agrarian & Economic	*Cultural & Educational*	
1910–1930 *(continued)*	Presidencies of A. Obregon and P. E. Calles	Create Indigenous Affairs Bureau in Ministry of Agriculture.	Assimilation occurs.	PRI (Institutional Revolutionary Party) formed. Agrarian reform pressures by indigenous groups.
1930–1940 Agrarian peace and Industrialization in Mexico	Presidencies of Portes Gil and Cárdenas. First Inter-American Congress of Indigenists held in Mexico.	Agrarian reform carried out and millions of hectares given to *ejidos* and *comunidades*. Bank for Ejido Credit created.	Instituto Nacional de Arqueología e Historia (INAH) created in 1938; Dept. for Indigenous Affairs becomes a Ministry. Thirty-three indigenous regions and boarding schools created. Use of indigenous language in school system proposed.	Students in boarding schools form Supreme Council of the Tarahumara (CSRT) and establish regional congresses of other groups. National Peasant Confederation formed within PRI.
1940–1970 Consolidation of the Revolution and modernization of country.	Presidencies of M. Avila Camacho, M. Alemán, A. Ruiz Cortines, and G. Díaz Ordaz. Large dams and other infrastructure constructed	Throughout period, lands continue to be given out. Indigenous centers for reform created in eleven regions in 1948.	Bilingual education introduced in 1963 as means to develop indigenous peoples and assist assimilation process.	Agreements with Yaqui and other groups signed. Resettlement of indigenous peoples due to infrastructure.

HISTORICAL PERIODS & DATES	NATIONAL ADMINISTRATION	PUBLIC POLICIES		IMPACTS & INDIGENOUS MOVEMENTS
		Agrarian & Economic	*Cultural & Educational*	
1940–1970 (continued)		Theory of assimilation and cultural integration dominates politics. Indigenous patrimony of Yaqui created in Mexquital Valley.	Experiments with bilingual education undertaken in the eleven indigenous regional centers.	Creation of National Confederation of Youth and Indigenous Communities (CNJCI). New organizations are formed for the protection of indigenous people. Student movement of 1968 alerts nation to need for more reforms. Guerrilla movements start in Chihuahua, Guerrero, Oaxaca, and Mexico City.
1970–1980	Presidencies of L. Echeverría and J. López Portillo	Twelve million hectares of land given in land reform. Sixty new indigenous centers created for national coverage. Large development programs initiated.	Department of Indigenous Education created and value of bilingual education recognized. Centers for study of social issues and indigenous issues created.	First indigenous congress in Chiapas, 1974. First Congress of Indigenous Peoples in Michoacán. National Confederation of Indigenous Peoples (CNPI) created after 1975 Congress.

HISTORICAL PERIODS & DATES	NATIONAL ADMINISTRATION	PUBLIC POLICIES		IMPACTS & INDIGENOUS MOVEMENTS
		Agrarian & Economic	*Cultural & Educational*	
1970–1980 *(continued)*				National Association of Indigenous Bilingual Professors is formed.
1980–1990 Initiate NAFTA dialogue and neoliberal reforms. Theories of marginality and poverty emerge.	Presidencies of J. López Portillo, M. de la Madrid, and C. Salinas de Gortari.	Slowdown of land reform programs. Development programs like Solidaridad are consolidated to address marginality and poverty issues. Agrarian support programs are reduced or cancelled.	Expansion of bilingual education coverage. Popular culture programs expanded for indigenous cultural heritage. Radio transmitters established in indigenous areas for transmission in local languages.	Conflict in Huasteca with new indigenous political organizations against state governments. New producers' organizations emerge to respond to fewer support programs. Multiparty alliances start to emerge. Many NGOs emerge to provide assistance in rural areas.

HISTORICAL PERIODS & DATES	NATIONAL ADMINISTRATION	PUBLIC POLICIES		IMPACTS & INDIGENOUS MOVEMENTS
		Agrarian & Economic	Cultural & Educational	
90–present nsolidate oliberal odel. 94 economic sis with rapid covery but rsistence strong equality.	Presidencies of C. Salinas de Gortari, E. Zedillo, V. Fox, and F. Calderón.	The reform of Article 27 of the Constitution by President Salinas permits transaction of *ejido* land, and the subsequent land-titling program (PROCEDE) of the Zedillo administration seeks to complete the land regularization and agrarian reform process. Solidarity program developed with new coverage of municipal funds. Oaxaca initiates a process of developing the Indigenous Peoples and Communities Rights Law.	Modification of Article 4 of the Constitution in 1992. New intellectual movements to recognize indigenous identity. Political parties begin to adopt a new discourse on indigenous affairs.	Emergence of peasant confederations in all political parties. Politicization of indigenous movements to promote legal reform. 1994—armed rebellion in Chiapas. 1996—San Andrés Accord signed and autonomous municipalities start to form.

APPENDIX 2.

Short Summary of International Events and Their Impact on Indigenous Political Movements

DATES, ENTITIES, AND LOCATIONS	EVENTS	RECOMMENDED POLICIES	IMPACTS
40 tzcuaro, Michoacán	Inter-American Indigenous Congress promoted by countries of region.	To respect and protect indigenous peoples for their development. Creation of national institutions for indigenous development.	Create the Indigenist Institute of Latin America in Mexico City as result of congress. Indigenous Institute created in 1948.
49 NESCO, meeting Paris, France	Meeting formulates the need for indigenous peoples to be addressed. Regional Center for Basic Education in Latin America created (Michoacán)	Train specialized education professionals for indigenous education.	Influence the educational politics in the continent.
59–1968 AS, ashington, D.C.	Organization of American States formulates an Applied Social Science Program in Mexico.	Train anthropologists and other applied professionals in the region.	Professionals work in Indigenous Institute and in indigenous education and with indigenous organizations.

DATES, ENTITIES, AND LOCATIONS	EVENTS	RECOMMENDED POLICIES	IMPACTS
1957 and 1989 International Labor Organization (ILO), New York	Convention 107 of 1957 for indigenous and tribal peoples and Convention 169 of 1989	Promote respect for indigenous culture and rights to indigenous identity and customs.	Mexico ratifies International Labor Organization Convention 169 and approves this as a law. Indigenous groups begin to make demands for its implementation.
1962–1965 Second Vatican Council, Rome	Vatican promotes liberation theology and organizes missions.	Promote indigenous rights through activities of Church authorities and leaders.	Church organizes indigenous peoples and a process of reflection, especially in Chiapas.
1994 United Nations, New York	Project for Global Declaration of Indigenous Peoples Rights	Human Rights Commission recognizes the urgent necessity of respecting indigenous rights, lands, and cultural resources.	Impact on national and state laws through reforms related to Article 4 of the Mexican Constitution.
1992 Inter-American Development Bank (IDB) Madrid, Spain	Creation of the Indigenous Fund (Fondo Indígena) in Bolivia with IDB support.	Establish a mechanism for channeling resources and technical assistance to indigenous communities and their organizations.	Mexico subscribes to this convention and provides financial resources for human development. World Bank creates Indigenous Peoples Training Program with International Development Forum (IDF) funds.

The San Andrés Accords, or the Law on Indian Rights and Culture, 1996

AGREEMENT

Regarding the documents:

"Joint declaration that the federal government and the EZLN shall submit to national debating and decision-making bodies"

"Joint proposals that the federal government and the EZLN agree to submit to national debating and decision-making bodies, in respect of point 1.4 of the rules of procedure"

"Commitments for Chiapas made by the state and federal governments and the EZLN, in respect of point 1.3 of the rules of procedure,"

stemming from the first part of the Resolutive Plenary Meeting on the topic "Indigenous Rights and Culture":

A. The Federal Government, through its delegation, expresses its acceptance of said documents.

B. The EZLN, through its delegation, expresses its acceptance of said documents. In regard to the issues on which it formulated, at the session on February 14, 1996, of this second part of the Resolutive Plenary Meeting, proposals for additions and substitutions or eliminations in the text of same, in accordance with the results of the consultations carried out by the EZLN, it expresses the following:

1. The delegation of the EZLN insists in pointing out the lack of solution to the grave national agrarian problem, and the need to amend Article 27 of the Constitution, which should reflect the

spirit of Emiliano Zapata, summarized in two basic demands: the land belongs to those who work it, and Land and Freedom (Document 2, "Joint proposals that the Federal Government and the EZLN agree to submit to national debating and decision-making bodies, in respect of point 1.4 of the Rules of Procedure," page 11, paragraph 5, "Constitutional and Legal Amendments," subparagraph B).

2. With regard to sustainable development, the delegation of the EZLN considers it insufficient for the government to compensate indigenous peoples for damage caused on their lands and territories, once the damage has been caused. There is a need to develop a policy of true sustainability that preserves the lands, territories, and natural resources of indigenous peoples, in short, that takes into account the social costs of development projects (Document 1, "Joint declaration that the Federal Government and the EZLN shall submit to national debating and decision-making bodies," page 3, in the subtitle "Principles of the new relationship," subparagraph 2).

3. In regard to the topic "Situation, Rights, and Culture of Indigenous Women," the delegation of the EZLN considers the present points of agreement insufficient. Owing to the triple oppression suffered by indigenous women—as women, as indigenous persons, and as poor persons—they demand the building of a new national society, with another economic, political, social, and cultural model that includes all Mexicans, both women and men (Document 3.2, "Actions and measures for Chiapas. Commitments and joint proposals of the State and Federal Governments and the EZLN," page 9).

4. In general terms, the delegation of the EZLN considers it necessary that, in each case, the times and terms in which the agreements should be put into practice be specified and that, to that end, the indigenous peoples and the pertinent authorities should program and schedule their implementation by mutual accord.

5. With regard to guarantees of full access to justice, the delegation of the EZLN considers that the need to appoint interpreters in all trials and lawsuits involving indigenous persons should not be ignored, ensuring that said interpreters are expressly accepted by the accused and that they know the language and are

familiar with the indigenous culture and legal system (Document 2, "Joint proposals that the Federal Government and the EZLN agree to submit to national debating and decision-making bodies, in respect of point 1.4 of the Rules of Procedure," page 6, subtitle "Guarantees of Full Access to Justice").

6. The delegation of the EZLN considers it essential that legislation be passed to protect the rights of migrants, both indigenous and nonindigenous, within and outside national borders (Document 1, "Joint declaration that the Federal Government and the EZLN shall submit to national debating and decision-making bodies," page 5, point 8, subtitle "Protecting Indigenous Migrants").

7. In order to strengthen the municipalities, the delegation of the EZLN considers that explicit commitments by the government are required to guarantee their access to adequate infrastructure, training, and economic resources (Document 2, "Joint proposals that the Federal Government and the EZLN agree to submit to national debating and decision-making bodies, in respect of point 1.4 of the Rules of Procedure," page 3).

8. With regard to the communications media, the delegation of the EZLN considers it necessary that access be guaranteed to reliable, timely, and sufficient information on the government's activities, as well as access by indigenous peoples to existing communications media, and that the right of indigenous peoples to have their own communications media (radio broadcasting, television, telephone, press, fax, communication radios, computers, and satellite access) be guaranteed (Document 2, "Joint proposals that the Federal Government and the EZLN agree to submit to national debating and decision-making bodies, in respect of point 1.4 of the Rules of Procedure," page 9, point 8, "Communications Media").

C. In regard to the parts of the documents to which subparagraph B refers, both delegations agree that, at the time that they identify by common accord during the dialogue, they shall exhaust negotiation efforts on same.

D. The parties shall submit to national debating and decision-making bodies and to other pertinent bodies the three accompanying documents, which contain the agreements and commitments reached by the parties.

E. Both parties assume the commitment to submit the present resolution to national debating and decision-making bodies and to the pertinent bodies of the state of Chiapas, in the understanding that the points indicated in subparagraph B should also be considered by said bodies as material resulting from the dialogue.

The present document and three documents that accompany it have been duly legalized as agreements under the terms of the Rules of Procedure and of the Law for Dialogue, Conciliation, and Dignified Peace in Chiapas, and are incorporated as such into the Agreement for Concord and Pacification with Justice and Dignity.

FEBRUARY 16, 1996

Notes

Introduction

1. See Assmann's "Collective Memory and Cultural Identity," *Das kulturelle Gedahtnis,* and "Kolektives Gedachnis und kulturelle Identitat."
2. Assmann, *Das kulturelle Gedahtnis,* 19.
3. Unknown author, "Cultural Memory," http://www.intergraphjournal.com/enhanced/articles/article%201/page17.html, pages 1–2.
4. Guzmán Bockler, "Memoria colectiva," 194.
5. Schuster and Boschert-Kimmig, *Hope against Hope,* 17.
6. Ibid., 34.
7. Dussel, *Ethics and the Theology of Liberation,* 123.

1. The Concept of Cultural Memory

1. Hirsch, *Genocide and the Politics of Memory,* 10–11.
2. Hinchman and Hinchman, *Memory, Identity, Community,* xvi.
3. Ibid., 1.
4. Ibid., 30.
5. Barthes, cited in ibid., 235.
6. Ibid.
7. Ibid., 265.
8. V. Schwarcz, *Bridge across Broken Time,* 4.
9. Schuster and Boschert-Kimmig, *Hope against Hope,* 68.
10. Davis, *Body as Spirit,* 151.
11. Schwarcz, *Bridge across Broken Time,* 13.
12. Becker, Annual address, 224.
13. Hirsch, *Genocide and the Politics of Memory,* 16–17.
14. Judith Miller, cited in Schwarcz, *Bridge across Broken Time,* 23.
15. Schwarcz, *Bridge across Broken Time,* 17.
16. We will be using the term "myth" to denote a cultural manner of understanding and explaining a particular cosmology and a way of revealing shared cultural values.
17. O'Flaherty, *Other People's Myths,* 27.
18. Wolf, "The Virgin of Guadalupe," 34–39.
19. Hoornaert, *The Memory of a Christian People,* 8–9.
20. Ibid., 9.

2. The Power of Image

1. The *Nican Mopohua* is found in a number of sources. I refer the readers to the work edited by Ernest Burrus, *The Oldest Copy of the Nican Mopohua*. The sources used for the interpretation of the significance of Our Lady of Guadalupe are Elizondo's *La Morenita* and Siller's *Flor y canto del Tepeyac*.

2. For a fuller presentation of this historical context, see Rodríguez, *Our Lady of Guadalupe*, 1−15.

3. This popular religious history is drawn from presentations given to visiting delegations by the Benedictine sisters of Guadalupe (de Christo Rey), Cuernavaca, Mexico.

4. Rodríguez, *Our Lady of Guadalupe*, 37.

5. Ibid., 38.

6. Ibid.

7. Ibid., 39.

8. Ibid.

9. Ibid.

10. Ibid., 40.

11. Elizondo, *La Morenita*, 85.

12. *A Handbook of Guadalupe*, 5.

13. Siller, *Flor y canto*, 50. All translations of Siller's work, which is unavailable in English, are mine.

14. Madsen, "Religious Syncretism," 377−378.

15. Ibid., 378.

16. Siller, *Flor y canto*, 61.

17. Metz, *Faith in History and Society*, 184.

18. Ibid., 184−185.

19. Ibid., 114.

20. Siller, *Flor y canto*.

21. Berryman, *Liberation Theology*, 9.

22. Siller, *Flor y canto*, 12−13.

23. See Ascheman, "Guadalupan Spirituality," 84.

24. Siller, *Flor y canto*, 11.

25. See Elizondo, *La Morenita*, 47−48; Rojas, *Nican Mopohua*; Siller, *Flor y canto*, 14. The translation of the quotations from the work by Mario Rojas is mine.

26. Cawley, *Guadalupe—from the Aztec Language*.

27. See Burrus, *Oldest Copy*, 3−4.

28. Ibid., 6−7.

29. Siller, *Flor y canto*, 32.

30. Ibid., 27.

31. Elizondo, *La Morenita*, 87−92.

32. Ibid., 88.

33. Ibid., 90.

34. Ibid.

35. Ibid., 91.

36. Metz, *Faith in History and Society*, 159.

37. "Salvation history" refers to the Judeo-Christian interpretation of God's involvement in human history.

38. This is a commonly quoted saying from Baba Dioum, the Senegalese conservationist.

39. Metz, *Faith in History and Society*, 159.

40. See Elizondo, *Galilean Journey*; *La Morenita*.

41. See Rodríguez, *Our Lady of Guadalupe*, 8, 17, 40; and Elizondo's recent publication *Guadalupe: Mother of the New Creation*.

42. John Donahue, public lecture at Mendocino College, California, August 1996.

43. Rodríguez-Holguín, "God Is Always Pregnant," 118.

44. "Us" has been expanded here to include any culturally identifiable group that has heard and been transformed by the Guadalupe event.

3. The Power of Secrecy and Ceremony

1. "Etic" refers to studying a culture from the perspective of an outsider, that is, using "preestablished categories for organizing and interpreting anthropological data, rather than categories recognized within the culture being studied" (Encarta World English Dictionary, 1999). The opposite term, "emic," refers to that view from someone from the culture. The terms are used extensively in the social sciences.

2. McGuire, *Politics and Ethnicity*, 5.

3. Sheridan, "How to Tell the Story," 179.

4. Lutes, "Yaqui Enclavement," 15.

5. By "ethnocide" we mean the process of eradicating the language, customs, and behaviors of an ethnic group.

6. By "genocide" we mean the actual killing off of a group of people.

7. The idea of a clan or kinship group claiming property rights over esoteric knowledge is a key element here. Other groups have a long documented history of such practices, among these the Aborigines of Australia and Northwest Coastal groups in North America. For nonindigenous people, a useful parallel here would be that of real property; that is, just as Western peoples often view real estate and heirlooms as elements that belong only to a particular family, many indigenous groups view particular realms of knowledge as private to a particular clan or family unit.

8. McGuire, *Politics and Ethnicity*, 73–74.

9. Fleming, *Spiritual Exercises*, 31–32.

10. See Anderson, "As Gentle as Lambs," and Morrison, "Baptism and Alliance."

11. See Steckley, "Warrior and Lineage," 379–509.

12. Fleming, *Spiritual Exercises*, 110–111.

13. Park, *Sacred Worlds*, 39.

14. Abicht, "Loyola, Lenin," 25.

15. Strasser, *Phenomenology of Feeling*, 17.

16. Abicht, "Loyola, Lenin," 28.

17. Richter, "Iroquois vs. Iroquois," 5.

18. Abicht, "Loyola, Lenin," 38.

19. While much has been written of Jesuit missions, there is little known about what these people actually based their lives on and what impelled them to choose such radically different lives. For a more in-depth discussion of the formation and ideology of the Jesuit missions, see Fortier, *Religion and Resistance*.

20. Butzer, *Americas before and after 1492*, 551.

21. See Acosta, cited in Butzer, *Americas before and after 1492*, 557.
22. Angrosino, "Culture Concept," 824.
23. See Morrison, "Baptism and Alliance," 418–420.
24. Steckley, "Warrior and Lineage," 478–509.
25. Spicer, *Perspectives*, 25.
26. Ibid., 12.
27. We use the term "horticultural" to designate farming without the use of draft animals or plow.
28. Reff, "Old World Diseases," 89.
29. Edward Spicer is the anthropologist most associated with Yaqui ethnography. Although he turned out an impressive array of publications regarding the Yaqui, there is much controversy now over his methods and interpretations. Ultimately, even Spicer admitted a lack of understanding or knowledge regarding the rituals of the Yaqui: "I do not know how to interpret it [i.e., a Yaqui ceremony]" ("Context," 324).
30. Spicer, *Cycles of Conquest*, 46.
31. Pérez de Ribas, *My Life*, 101.
32. Spicer, *Cycles of Conquest*, 48.
33. See Pérez de Ribas, *My Life*, 103–109, for a vivid description of a battle between the Spaniards and thousands of Yaqui and of the latter's tremendous battlefield abilities.
34. Ibid., 102.
35. Reff, "Old World Diseases," 92.
36. Spicer, *Cycles of Conquest*, 47–52.
37. Pérez de Ribas, *History*, 108.
38. Ibid., 110, 129.
39. Spicer, *Perspectives*, 32.
40. Ibid., 33–35.
41. In order to receive final vows as a Jesuit priest, each Jesuit in New Spain had to prove proficiency in at least two languages of the New World. They were regularly re-examined for these competencies.
42. Pérez de Ribas, *History*, 125–131. In addition to Pérez de Ribas, Frs. Tomás Basilio, Juan de Ardenas, Diego Bandersnipe, Pedro Méndez, Angelo Balestra, and others worked in the Yaqui Jesuit mission. At the height of the mission activity, each Jesuit was responsible for over four thousand Indians.
43. McGuire, *Politics and Ethnicity*, 5.
44. Pérez de Ribas, *History*, 116. The crosses that the Indians carried were mistaken by the missionaries as crucifixes, signifying the Indians' readiness to become Christian. Rather, the crosses were, and continue to be, indigenous symbols to ward off evil and to bring good to the household or holder.
45. Spicer, *Perspectives*, 58–59.
46. These cults continue to vivify the Yaqui cultural landscape, and they are the main organizers of the ritual calendar. Again, it would be inappropriate for us to explain the structure and organization of these entities.
47. Hu-DeHart, *Yaqui Resistance and Survival*, 4.
48. Spicer, *Perspectives*, 27.
49. Established in South America by Jesuits from 1609 to 1767, "*reducciones*" were communal mission villages where the Jesuits taught the arts to the indigenous people

and developed agriculture and cattle ranches. They were never restored after the Jesuits were ordered to leave the New World and their missions (Hardon, *Modern Catholic Dictionary*). See also Richter, "Iroquois vs. Iroquois," and McNaspy, *Lost Cities of Paraguay*.

50. Burns, *Jesuits and the Indian Wars*, 41.

51. For historical accounts of Yaqui dispersal and efforts to exterminate them, please refer to Spicer, "Context of the Yaqui Easter Ceremony," *Cycles of Conquest, Perspectives*, and *The Yaquis*; Sheridan, "How to Tell the Story"; and Hu-DeHart, *Missionaries, Miners, and Indians, Yaqui Resistance and Survival*, and "Yaqui Resistance to Mexican Expansion."

52. Lutes, "Yaqui Enclavement," 12–13.

53. Juan Banderas, so named because he carried a flag (*bandera*) depicting the Virgin of Guadalupe into battle, led an Indian resistance movement in Sonora, which was defeated in 1832; see Spicer, *Perspectives*, 8.

54. Zoontjens, *Brief History*, 7.

55. McGuire, *Politics and Ethnicity*, 5.

56. Zoontjens, *Brief History*, 8.

57. Rev. Wasielski and the parish of Our Lady of Guadalupe, Annual Easter Program, 2000.

58. V. Turner, *Forest of Symbols*.

59. Jesuit Archives of New Spain, Vol. 2, Book 39.

60. Sands, "The Singing Tree," 356.

61. Sheridan, "How to Tell the Story," 179.

62. Hu-DeHart, *Yaqui Resistance and Survival*, 3.

63. Spicer, "Context," 313.

64. McGuire, *Politics and Ethnicity*, 1.

65. Spicer, "Context," 324.

66. Spicer, for example, suggests that the plays the Jesuits used as teaching tools, including passion plays from the Old World, combined indigenous and religious rituals ("Context," 318).

67. Painter, *With Good Heart*, 349.

68. Sands, "The Singing Tree," 359–362. Sands provides a very good analysis of the melding of origin myths and the reconciliation of precontact to contact religious explanations.

69. Vows are taken to fulfill personal obligations to the Lord, such as a return to good health, the success of an endeavor, and so on. These are very important, and often take from a year to their whole life to fulfill.

4. The Power of Narrative

1. The Farabundo Martí National Liberation Front (in Spanish: Frente Farabundo Martí para la Liberación Nacional, or FMLN) was a Marxist coalition guerrilla movement that emerged in El Salvador in 1980 and has today become a major political party of the country, drawing membership from both old radicals and more moderate leftists. The party was successful in forming coalitions with a variety of other leftist parties, and was the defining party of resistance to ARENA (Nationalist Republican Alliance) during the oppressions.

2. Dear, *Oscar Romero*, 7.

3. Ibid., 14.

4. Juan Carlos, personal interview, November 1998.

5. This was to many a very enlightening moment, for Romero had been a vocal critic of the Puebla proceedings. His reference here is to the documents that came out of the Third General Conference of the Latin American Episcopate in Puebla de los Angeles, Mexico, February 1979.

6. Romero, "Church's Option for the Poor," Louvain, Belgium, February 2, 1980, in *Oscar Romero*, 175–177.

7. Ibid.

8. Ibid., 176.

9. Ibid., 177.

10. Interview with the staff of Equipo Maíz, November 1998.

11. Interview with "Carlos" at Radio UCA, November 1998.

12. In fact, disappearances and murders continue to haunt the Salvadoran people, with as many as 20,000 disappeared since 1989. And, in the spring of 2005, a security guard at the Lutheran University, known to be another important spot for liberation theology, was found murdered, hung from a tree.

13. Romero, address at Louvain University, February 2, 1980; Walsh, *Oscar Romero*, 178.

5. The Power of Syncretism/Inculturation

1. "Syncretism" is a term used by social scientists to refer to the process by which foreign cultural elements are fused into and redefined by another culture.

2. "Inculturation" is a term that has been in use by Christian groups during the last thirty years. "A short definition of inculturation is: the on-going dialogue between faith and culture or cultures. More fully, it is the creative and dynamic relationship between the Christian message and a culture or cultures" (Shorter, *Toward a Theology of Inculturation*, 11).

3. "*Jtatik*," which means "our father," is a term of respect among the Tzeltal.

4. Story collected at a gathering of Tzeltal and Jesuits, Ch'ich, Mexico, 2003.

5. "Autochthonous community" is a term taken from the Catholic Church's concept in recent years that the "seeds of the faith" were present in every culture prior to the encounter with Christianity (Gremillion, *Gospel of Peace and Justice*, 5–21). The term itself comes from the Greek, meaning "from the land" (*auto* = "self, proper," and *chthon* = "land").

6. Zatyrka, "Formation," 226.

7. Ibid., 233.

8. http://www.houstonculture.org/mexico/chiapas.html

9. http://library.utoronto.ca/pcs/eps/chiapsl.html

10. Zatyrka, "Formation," 177.

11. See, for example, "De unico Evangelizandi modo," in ibid., 177–178.

12. Along with the Spanish Conquest and exploration came Spanish customs and traditions. The Spaniards brought with them a system of forced labor called the "*encomienda*." An *encomienda* was a gift from the Spanish Crown to a Spaniard that gave him a restricted set of property rights over Indian labor. The Spaniard, or *encomendero*,

extracted tributes from the Indians in the form of goods, metals, money, and labor. In return for these, the *encomendero* was supposed to provide the Indians with protection and instruction in the Christian faith. They also promised to defend the area and to pay a tax to the Crown.

13. http://www.travelchiapas.com/about/about-5.php

14. See, for instance, Gary Palmer's work on indigenous languages and place, *Toward a Theory of Cultural Linguistics*.

15. Zatyrka, "Formation," 233.

16. Villa Rojas, "Notas," 197.

17. During our stays with the Tzeltal, the meals consisted of maize tortillas and beans.

18. These cooperatives include a farm that is using natural indigenous methods to raise maize and other crops, as well as cattle, and a cooperative that enables coffee growers to sell their products at a fair price.

19. For further information on the Omaha kin terms, see Fox, *Kinship and Marriage*, 225.

20. See, for instance, Stone, *Kinship and Gender*.

21. Zatyrka, "Formation," 229.

22. Ibid., 234.

23. Ibid., 239–242.

24. Maurer, *Los Tseltales*, 445.

25. Zatyrka, "Formation," 189. About 400,000 people, representing over one thousand Indian communities, participated in the year-long preparation for this congress.

26. Ibid., 189, 190, 191.

27. Ibid., 197–198.

28. Ibid., 201–203.

29. Maurer, unpublished manuscript, 1.

30. Maurer, personal communication, October 2005.

31. According to Maurer, these punishments represent some kind of amends for the fault that has led to the illness, often a staged ceremonial whipping, for example.

32. The importance of candles and copal, or incense, is something to be noted. The Tzeltal believe the candles represent the light of the soul and the prayer that is being said; the incense is the prayer rising to God. When a candle is lit in prayer, people do not leave until the candle has burned down and been extinguished.

33. The Jesuits of the mission have petitioned Rome to allow the married deacons to be ordained to the priesthood, and to get permission to allow widowed deacons to remarry and retain their role as deacons. Although the official Church does decree that a deacon can only be married once, any particular deacon can petition Rome for an exception to that policy. What the Tzeltal would like, however, is recognition of their particular situation and cultural practices. This is not unusual for indigenous people, either. For example, Jesuits working with the Yupik of Alaska regularly petition Rome for exceptions to the marriage rule.

34. Jeanne Berwick, personal communication, September 2005.

35. Eugenio Maurer, personal communication, October 2005.

36. Ibid.

6. Final Thoughts

1. Schreiter, *The New Catholicity,* 29.

2. Assmann, "Collective Memory," 125.

3. Jonathan Boyarin does point out that Halbwachs failed to place cultural memory in a historical context, but Halbwachs's work suggests the importance of history, nevertheless. See Boyarin, *Remapping Memory,* 24.

4. Ibid., 126.

5. Ibid., 129–130.

Bibliography

Abicht, Ludo. "Loyola, Lenin, and the Road to Liberation." *Monthly Review* 36 (October 1984): 24–31.

Accords of San Andrés. http://www.ezln.org/san andres/acuerdos.en.htm (2006).

Acosta, José de. *Historia natural y moral de las Indias* [1590]. In *Obras del P. José de Acosta de la Compañía de Jesús*, ed. Francisco Mateos. Biblioteca de Autores Españoles (continuación), 73:3–247. Madrid: Ediciones Atlas, 1954.

Adams, Walter R., ed. "Social Structure in Pilgrimage and Prayer: Tzeltels as Lords and Servants." In *Pilgrimage in Latin America*, 109–121. Westport, CT: Greenwood, 1991.

Alegre, Francisco Xavier. *Historia de la Provincia de la Compañía de Jesús de Nueva España*. Vol. 9. Rome: Jesuit Historical Institute, 1956.
———. *Historia de la Provincia de la Compañía de Jesús de Nueva España*. Vol. 16. Rome: Jesuit Historical Institute, 1959.

Alexander, Jeffrey C. "Introduction: Durkheimian Sociology and Cultural Studies Today." In *Durkheimian Sociology: Cultural Studies*, ed. Jeffrey C. Alexander, 1–21. Cambridge: Cambridge University Press, 1988.

Alexy, Trudi. *The Mezuzah in the Madonna's Foot*. New York: Simon and Schuster, 1995.

Alonso, Ana Maria. "The Effects of Truth: Pre-representations of the Past and the Imagining of the Community." *Journal of Historical Sociology* 1 (1988): 33–57.

Anderson, Karen. "As Gentle as Lambs: Images of Huron and Montagnai-Haskapi Women in the Writings of the Seventeenth-Century Jesuits." *Canadian Review of Sociology and Anthropology* 25, no. 4 (1985): 560–576.

Angrosino, Michael V. "The Culture Concept and the Mission of the Roman Catholic church." *American Anthropologist* 96, no. 4 (1992): 824–832.

Ascheman, Thomas J. "Guadalupan Spirituality for Cross-cultural Missionaries." M.A. thesis, Catholic Theological Union at Chicago, 1983.

Assmann, Jan. "Collective Memory and Cultural Identity." *New German Critique* 65 (Spring–Summer 1995): 124–135.

———. *Das kulturelle Gedahtnis: Schrift, Erinnerung und politische Identitain fraen Hochkulturen.* Munich: Beck, 1992.

———. "Kolektives Gedachnis und kulturelle Identitat." In *Kultur und Gedahnis*, ed. Jan Assmann and T. Holscher, 9–19. Frankfurt: Suhrkamp, 1988.

———. "Stein und Zeit: Das 'monumentale' Gedachtnis der altagyptischen Kultur." In *Kultur und Gedahnis*, ed. Jan Assmann and T. Holscher, 87–114. Frankfurt: Suhrkamp, 1988.

Avruch, Kevin, and Walter P. Zenner, ed. *Critical Essays on Israeli Society, Religion, and Government.* Albany: State University of New York Press, 1997.

Bailey, Helen Miller, and Abraham P. Nasatir. *Latin America: The Development of Its Civilization.* New Jersey: Prentice Hall, 1968.

Bancroft, Hubert Howe. *History of the North Mexican States and Texas.* 2 vols. San Francisco: The History Company, 1884.

Bannon, John Francis. *Missionary Frontier in Sonora, 1620–1687.* New York: U.S. Catholic Historical Society, 1955.

Barker, William B. "Eyewitness at Vicam Station: Bill Barker Remembers the Yaqui Revolt of 1926." *Journal of Arizona History* 37, no. 4 (1996): 357–369.

Bartlett, F. C. *Remembering.* Cambridge: Cambridge University Press, 1932.

Bausch, William J. *Storytelling: Imagination and Faith.* Mystic, Conn.: Twenty-Third Publications, 1984.

Becker, Carl. Annual address of the president of the American Historical Association, delivered at Minneapolis, December 29, 1931. *American Historical Review* 37, no. 2 (January 1932): 221–236.

Belli, Robert F., Howard Schuman, Steven Blixt, and Benita Jackson. "The Misremembering of Important Past Events." Paper presented at the American Association for Public Opinion Research conference, Ft. Lauderdale, Fla., 1995.

Berryman, Philip. *Liberation Theology: The Essential Facts about the Revolutionary Movement in Latin America and Beyond.* New York: I. B. Taurus and Co., 1987.

Billings, Dwight B. "Religion as Opposition: A Gramscian Analysis." *American Journal of Sociology* 96, no. 1 (1990): 1–31.

Bloch, Maurice E. F. *How We Think They Think: Anthropological Approaches to Cognition, Memory, and Literacy.* Boulder, CO: Westview Press, 1998.

Boyarin, Jonathan, ed. *Remapping Memory: The Politics of Timespace.* Minneapolis: University of Minnesota Press, 1994.

Brown, Kenneth. "Polish Jews in Paris: The Ethnography of Memory." *American Anthropologist* 95 (1993): 239.

Burns, Robert Ignatius. *The Jesuits and the Indian Wars of the Northwest.* Moscow: University of Idaho Press, 1960.

Burrus, Ernest J. *The Oldest Copy of the Nican Mopohua.* CARA Studies on Popular

Devotion Vol. 4; Guadalupan Studies No. 4. Washington, D.C.: Center for Applied Research in the Apostolate (CARA), 1981. Pamphlet.

———. *The Basic Bibliography of the Guadalupan Apparitions.* CARA Studies on Popular Devotion Vol. 4. Washington, D.C.: Center for Applied Research in the Apostolate (CARA), 1983. Pamphlet.

Butzer, Karl W., ed. *The Americas before and after 1492: An Introduction to Current Geographical Research.* Annals of the Association of American Geographers 82, no. 3. Boston: Blackwell, 1992.

———. "From Columbus to Acosta: Science, Geography, and the New World." In *The Americas before and after 1492,* ed. Karl W. Butzer, 543–565. Annals of the Association of American Geographers 82, no. 3. Boston: Blackwell, 1992.

Carlyle, Thomas. *Past and Present.* New York: Charles Scribner's Sons, 1918.

Cawley, Martinua. *Guadalupe—from the Aztec Language.* CARA Studies in Popular Devotion, no. 2; *Guadalupan Studies,* no. 6. Lafayette, OR: Guadalupe Abbey, 1984.

Chevalier, Francois, ed. *Instrucciones a los hermanos jesuitas administradores de haciendas.* Mexico City: Universidad Nacional Autónoma de México, 1950.

Collier, George Allan. *Basta!: Land and the Zapatista Rebellion in Chiapas.* Oakland, CA: The Institute for Food and Development, 1994.

Connerton, Paul. *How Societies Remember.* Cambridge: Cambridge University Press, 1989.

Csikzentmihalyi, Mihaly, and Fausto Massimini. "On the Psychological Selection of Biocultural Information." *New Ideas in Psychology* 3 (1985): 115–138.

Davis, Charles. *Body as Spirit: The Nature of Religious Feeling.* New York: Seabury Press, 1976.

Dear, John. *Oscar Romero and the Non-Violent Struggle for Justice.* Erie, PA: Pax Christi, 1991.

"Demography of Chiapas." http://www.travelchiapas.com/about-5.php, Vol. 2005: Travel Chiapas, 2004.

Dunne, Peter Masten. *Early Jesuit Missions in Tarahumara.* Berkeley: University of California Press, 1948.

———. *Pioneer Black Robes on the West Coast.* Berkeley: University of California Press, 1940.

Duran, Livie I., ed. *Introduction to Chicano Studies: A Reader.* 2d ed. New York: Prentice Hall, 1982.

Dussel, Enrique. *Ethics and the Theology of Liberation.* Translated by Bernard F. McWilliams. Maryknoll, NY: Orbis Books, 1978.

Edgerton, Gary. "Ken Burns's America: Style, Authorship, and Cultural Memory." *Journal of Popular Film and Television* 21 (Summer 1993): 50.

Eliade, Mircea. *Patterns in Comparative Religion.* New York and Cleveland: World Publishing Company, 1971.

Elizondo, Virgilio P. *Galilean Journey: The Mexican-American Promise*. Maryknoll, NY: Orbis Books, 1983.

——. *Guadalupe: Mother of the New Creation*. Maryknoll, NY: Orbis Books, 1997.

——. *La Morenita: Evangelizer of the Americas*. San Antonio, TX: Mexican-American Cultural Center, 1980.

Evers, Larry, and Felipe S. Molina. *Yaqui Deer Songs, Maso Bwikam: Native American Poetry*. Tucson: University of Arizona Press, 1987.

Farris, Nancy M. *Crown and Clergy in Colonial Mexico, 1759–1821: The Crisis of Ecclesiastical Privilege*. London: University of London, Athlone Press, 1968.

Fentress, James, and Chris Wickham. *Social Memory*. Oxford: Blackwell, 1992.

Fleming, David. *The Spiritual Exercises of St. Ignatius: A Literal Translation and a Contemporary Reading*. St. Louis, Mo.: St. Louis Institute of Jesuit Sources, 1998.

Fortier, Ted N. "Piercing Hearts: Coeur d'Alene Indians and Jesuit Priests on the Columbia Plateau." Ph.D. diss., Washington State University, 1995.

——. *Religion and Resistance in the Encounter between Coeur d'Alene Indians and Jesuit Missionaries*. New York: Mellen, 2002.

Fox, Robin. *Kinship and Marriage: An Anthropological Perspective*. New York: Cambridge University Press, 1967.

Frisch, Michael. "American History and the Structures of Collective Memory: A Modest Exercise in Empirical Iconography." *Journal of American History* 75 (March 1989): 1130.

García, Luis Navarro. *Sonora y Sinaloa en el Siglo XVII*. Sevilla: Consejo Superior de Investigaciones Científicas, 1967.

Garrison, Charles E. *Two Different Worlds: Christian Absolutes and the Relativism of Social Science*. Newark, N.J.: Associated University Press, 1988.

Geertz, Clifford. *The Interpretation of Cultures*. New York: Basic Books, 1973.

Goldberg, Michael. *Theology and Narrative: A Critical Introduction*. Nashville, Tenn.: Abingdon Press, 1982.

Gossen, Gary H., ed. *South and Meso-American Native Spirituality: From the Cult of the Feather Serpent to the Theology of Liberation*. In collaboration with Miguel León-Portilla. New York: Crossroads, 1993.

Gradie, Charlotte May. "Jesuit Missions in Spanish North America, 1566–1623." Ph.D. diss., University of Connecticut, 1990.

Greene, Gayle. "Feminist Fiction and the Uses of Memory." *Signs: Journal of Women in Culture and Society* 16, no. 2 (1991): 290–321.

Gremillion, Joseph. *The Gospel of Peace and Justice: Catholic Social Teaching since Pope John*. Maryknoll, N.Y.: Orbis Books, 1976.

Gusfield, Joseph R., and Jerzy Michalowicz. "Secular Symbolism: Studies of Ritual,

Ceremony, and the Symbolic Order in Modern Life." *Annual Review of Sociology* 10 (1984): 417–435.

Guzmán Bockler, Carlos. "Memoria colectiva, identidad histórica y conciencia étnica en Guatemala." *Revista Mexicana de Ciencias Políticas y Sociales* (Mexico City) 27, no. 103 (1981): 193–208.

Halbwachs, Maurice. *The Collective Memory*. New York: Harper, 1980. Originally published in 1950.

———. *On Collective Memory*. Translated by Lewis Coser. Chicago: University of Chicago Press, 1992.

A Handbook of Guadalupe. Kenosha, WI: Franciscan Marystories Press, 1974.

Harding, Sandra. *Whose Science? Whose Knowledge? Thinking from Women's Lives*. Ithaca, NY: Cornell University Press, 1991.

Hardon, John. *Modern Catholic Dictionary*. Garden City, N.Y.: Doubleday, 1980.

Hauser, Kornelia. "Feminist Literature as an Element of a Cultural Memory." *Argument* 30 (1988): 326–337.

Hinchman, Lewis P., and Sandra K. Hinchman. *Memory, Identity, Community—the Idea of Narrative in the Human Sciences*. Albany: State University of New York Press, 1997.

Hirsch, Herbert. *Genocide and the Politics of Memory*. Chapel Hill and London: University of North Carolina Press, 1995.

Hirsch, Maurice. "Family Pictures: Maus, Mourning, and Post-Memory." *Discourse: Theoretical Studies in Media and Culture* 15, no. 2 (1992–1993): 3–29.

"History of Chiapas." http://www.houstonculture.org/mexico/chiapas.html, Vol. 2005, 2004.

Hoffman, Ronan. *Pioneer Theories of Missiology*. Washington, D.C.: Catholic University of America, 1960.

Hoornaert, Eduardo. *The Memory of a Christian People*. Maryknoll, N.Y.: Orbis Books, 1988.

Hu-DeHart, Evelyn. *Missionaries, Miners, and Indians: Spanish Contact with the Yaqui Nation of Northwestern New Spain, 1533–1820*. Tucson: University of Arizona, 1981.

———. *Yaqui Resistance and Survival: The Struggle for Land and Autonomy 1821–1910*. Madison: University of Wisconsin Press, 1984.

———. "Yaqui Resistance to Mexican Expansion." In *The Indian in Latin American History: Resistance, Resilience, and Acculturation*, ed. John E. Kicza, 141–169. Wilmington, Del.: Scholarly Resources, 1993.

"Human Rights in Chiapas." http://www.library.utoronto.ca/pcs/eps/chiapas.htm, Vol. 2005: University of Toronto, 2004.

Ibarra, Jorge Luis. *Propiedad agraria y sistema político en México*. Sonora, Mexico: Colegio de Sonora, 1989.

Isenberg, Noah. *Between Redemption and Doom: The Strains of German-Jewish Modernism*. Lincoln: University of Nebraska Press, 1999.

Jackson, Robert H. *Indian Population Decline: The Missions of Northwestern New Spain, 1687–1840*. Albuquerque: University of New Mexico Press, 1994.

Jesuit Archives of New Spain. Vol. 2, Book 39. Microfiche file, St. Louis University, St. Louis, Mo.

Knapp, Steven. "Collective Memory and the Actual Past." *Representations* 26 (Spring 1989): 134–147.

Kolaz, Thomas M. "Tohono O'odham Fariseos at the Village of Kawori'k." *Journal of the Southwest* 39, no. 1 (1997): 59–77.

Kragh, Hekge. *Quantum Generations: A History of Physics in the Twentieth Century*. Princeton: Princeton University Press, 1999.

Krausz, Michael, ed. *Relativism: Interpretation and Confrontation*. Notre Dame: University of Notre Dame Press, 1989.

Kurtz, Donald V. "The Virgin of Guadalupe and the Politics of Becoming Human." *Journal of Anthropological Research* 38 (Summer 1982): 192–210.

Lachieze-Rey, Marc. *Cosmology: A First Course*. Translated by John Simmons. Cambridge: Cambridge University Press, 1995.

Larson, Magali S. "Reading Architecture in the Holocaust Memorial Museum: A Method and an Empirical Illustration." In *From Sociology to Cultural Studies: New Perspectives*, ed. Elizabeth Long, 62–90. Malden, Mass.: Blackwell Publishers, 1997.

Levine, Robert. *A Geography of Time*. New York: Basic Books, 1997.

Lewis, Pierce. "The Future of Our Past: Our Clouded Vision of Historic Preservation." *Pioneer American* 7, no. 1 (1975): 1–20.

Lutes, Steven V. "Yaqui Enclavement: The Effects of an Experimental Indian Policy in Northwestern Mexico." In *Ejidos and Regions of Refuge in Northwestern Mexico*, ed. Phil Weigard, 11–22. Anthropological Papers of the University of Arizona, Vol. 46. Tucson: University of Arizona Press, 1987.

MacEoin, Gary. *The People's Church: Bishop Samuel Ruiz of Mexico and Why He Matters*. New York: Crossroads, 1996.

Madsen, William. "Religious Syncretism." In *Social Anthropology*, Vol. 3, *Handbook of Middle American Indians*, ed. Manning Nash, 369–391. Austin: University of Texas Press, 1967.

Maines, David R., Noreen M. Sugurue, and Michael A. Katovich. "The Sociological Impact of G. H. Mead's Theory of the Past." *American Sociological Review* 48 (1983): 161–173.

Markovits, Andrei S. *The German Predicament: Memory and Power in the New Europe*. Ithaca: Cornell University Press, 1997.

Maurer, Eugenio. *Los Tseltales*. Mexico City: Centro de Estudios Educativos, 1983.

——. "The Tzeltal Maya-Christian Synthesis." In *South and Meso-American Native Spirituality*, ed. Gary Gossen, 228–250. New York: Crossroads, 1993.

McGuire, Thomas R. *Politics and Ethnicity on the Rio Yaqui: Potam Revisited.* Tucson: University of Arizona Press, 1986.

McNaspy, Clement J. *Lost Cities of Paraguay: Art and Architecture of the Jesuit Reductions, 1607–1767.* Chicago: Loyola University Press, 1981.

Metz, Johann Baptist. *Faith in History and Society: Toward a Practical Fundamental Theology.* New York: Crossroads, 1980.

Miles, Margaret. *Image as Insight.* Boston: Beacon Press, 1985.

Monumentos Guadalupanos, Nican Mopohua. Mexico, ca. 1548, series 1. New York: Public Library of New York City, Ramírez Collection.

Morris, Walter. *Living Maya.* New York: Harry N. Abrams, 1987.

Morrison, Kenneth M. "Baptism and Alliance: The Symbolic Mediations of Religious Syncretism." *Ethnohistory* 37, no. 4 (1990): 416–435.

Nelson, Cary, and Walter Kalaidjian. *Repression and Recovery: Modern American Poetry and the Politics of Cultural Memory.* Madison: University of Wisconsin Press, 1989.

Nora, Pierre. "Between Memory and History: Les Lieux de Memoire." *Representations* 26 (Spring 1989): 7–25.

O'Flaherty, Wendy Doniger. *Other People's Myths.* New York: Macmillan, 1988.

Painter, Muriel Thayer. *Easter at Pascua Village.* Tucson: University of Arizona Press, 1960.
——. *Faith, Flowers, and Fiestas: The Yaqui Indian Year.* Tucson: University of Arizona Press, 1962.
——. *With Good Heart: Yaqui Beliefs and Ceremonies in Pascua Village.* Tucson: University of Arizona Press, 1986.

Palmer, Gary. *Toward a Theory of Cultural Linguistics.* Austin: University of Texas Press, 1996.
——. "Where the Muskrats Are: The Semantic Structure of Coeur d'Alene Place Names." *Anthropological Linguistics* 32 (1990): 263–294.

Park, Chris. *Sacred Worlds: An Introduction to Geography and Religion.* New York and London: Routledge, 1994.

Pérez de Ribas, Andrés. *History of the Triumphs of Our Holy Faith against the Most Barbarous and Fierce People of the New World.* Translated by Daniel Reff and Richard Danford. Tucson: University of Arizona Press, 1990. Original published in 1644.
——. *My Life among the Savage Nations of New Spain.* Los Angeles: Ward Ritchie Press, 1968.

Perkins, David. "Repression and Recovery: Modern American Poetry and the Politics of Cultural Memory." *Style* 25 (1991): 156.

Polzer, Charles W. *Rules and Precepts of the Jesuit Missions of Northwestern New Spain*. Tucson: University of Arizona Press, 1976.

Rees, Billie DeWalt, Martha Rees, and Arthur D. Murphy. *The End of Agrarian Reform in Mexico: Transformation of Rural Mexico*. San Diego: University of San Diego Press, 1994.

Reff, Daniel T. "Old World Diseases and the Dynamics of Indian and Jesuit Relations in Northwestern New Spain, 1520–1660." In *Ejidos and Regions of Refuge in Northwestern Mexico*, ed. N. Ross Crumrine and Phil C. Weigand, 46:85–93. Tucson: University of Arizona Press, 1987.

Reynolds, Mary Stephanie. "Yaqui Deer Songs: Maso Bwikam, Native American Poetry." *American Indian Quarterly* 14, no. 2 (1990): 204.

Richter, Daniel K. "Iroquois vs. Iroquois: Jesuit Mission and Christianity in Village Politics, 1642–1686." *Ethnohistory* 32, no. 1 (1986): 1–16.

Robinson, Alfred Eugene. "Beneath the Masks of the Pahkola: Survival, Continuity, and Renaissance in the Body of the Yaqui Tradition." Master's thesis, University of California Los Angeles, 1992.
———. "The Legend of the First Pahkola: Structure and Counter-structure in a Syncretistic Yaqui Myth." *Wicazo sa Review* 9, no. 1 (1993): 1–3.

Roca, Paul M. *Spanish Jesuit Churches in Mexico's Tarahumara*. Tucson: University of Arizona Press, 1979.

Rodríguez, Jeanette. *Our Lady of Guadalupe: Faith and Empowerment among Mexican American Women*. Austin: University of Texas Press, 1994.

Rodríguez-Holguín, Jeanette. "God Is Always Pregnant." In *The Divine Mosaic: Women's Images of the Sacred Power*, ed. Theresa King, 111–126. St. Paul, Minn.: YES International Publishers, 1994.

Rojas, Mario, trans. *Nican Mopohua*. Translation from Nahuatl to Spanish. Huejutla, Hidalgo, Mexico: N.p., 1978.

Romero, Oscar. "Church's Option for the Poor." In *Oscar Romero, Voice of the Voiceless: The Four Pastoral Letters and Other Statements*, trans. Michael J. Walsh, 175–177. Maryknoll, N.Y.: Orbis Books, 1985.

Rosenman, Stanly, and Irving Handelsman. "The Collective Past, Group Psychology and Personal Narrative: Shaping Jewish Identity by Memoirs of the Holocaust." *American Journal of Psychoanalysis* 50 (June 1990): 151–170.

Ross, John. *Rebellion from the Roots: Indian Uprising in Chiapas*. Monroe, Maine: Common Courage Press, 1995.

Sands, Kathleen M. "The Singing Tree: Dynamics of a Yaqui Myth." *American Quarterly* 35, no. 4 (1983): 355–375.

Schreiter, Robert J. *The New Catholicity: Theology between the Global and Local*. Maryknoll, NY: Orbis Books, 1998.

Schuman, Howard, Robert F. Belli, and Katherine Bischoping. "The Generational Basis of Knowledge." In *Collective Memories of Political Events: Social Psychological Perspectives*, ed. Dario Paez, James W. Pennebaker, and Bernard Rime, 47–78. Hillsdale, NJ: Lawrence Erlbaum, 1997.

Schuman, Howard, and Jacqueline Scott. "Generations and Collective Memories." *American Sociological Review* 54 (1989): 359–381.

Schuster, Ekkehard, and Reinhold Boschert-Kimmig. *Hope against Hope: Johann Baptist Metz and Elie Wiesel Speak Out on the Holocaust.* New York: Paulist Press, 1999.

Schwarcz, Vera. *Bridge across Broken Time: Chinese and Jewish Cultural Memory.* New Haven and London: Yale University Press, 1998.

Schwartz, Barry. "Iconography and Collective Memory: Lincoln's Image in the American Mind." In *Sociological Quarterly* 32 (1991): 301–319.
———. "Rereading the Gettysburg Address: Social Change and Collective Memory." *Qualitative Sociology* 19, no. 3 (1996): 395–423.
———. "The Social Context of Commemoration: A Study in Collective Memory." *Social Forces* 61 (1982): 374–402.

Sheridan, Thomas E. "How to Tell the Story of a 'People without History': Narrative versus Ethno-historical Approaches to the Study of the Yaqui Indians through Time." *Journal of the Southwest* 30, no. 2 (1988): 168–189.

Shorter, Aylward. *Toward a Theology of Inculturation.* Maryknoll, N.Y.: Orbis Books, 1988.

Shweder, Richard A., and Robert A. LeVine, eds. *Cultural Theory: Essays on Mind, Self, and Emotion.* New York: Cambridge University Press, 1984.

Siller, Clodomiro A. *Flor y canto del Tepeyac: Historia de las apariciones de Santa María Guadalupe.* Mexico City: Servir, 1981.

Spicer, Edward H. "Context of the Yaqui Easter Ceremony." In *New Dimensions in Dance Research: Anthropology and Dance—The American Indian*, ed. Thomas Comstock, 318–346. New York: Committee on Research in Dance, 1972.
———. *Cycles of Conquest: The Impact of Spain, Mexico, and the United States on the Indians of the Southwest, 1533–1960.* Tucson: University of Arizona Press, 1976.
———, ed. *Perspectives in American Indian Culture Change.* Chicago: University of Chicago Press, 1961.
———. *The Yaquis: A Cultural History.* Tucson: University of Arizona, 1980.

Steckley, John. "The Warrior and Lineage: Jesuit Use of Iroquoian Images to Communicate Christianity." *Ethnohistory* 39, no. 4 (1995): 379–509.

Stone, Linda. *Kinship and Gender.* Boulder, Colo.: Westview Press, 2000.

Strasser, Stephen. *The Phenomenology of Feeling.* Pittsburgh, Pa.: Duquesne University Press, 1977.

Teres, Harvey. "Repression, Recovery, Renewal: The Politics of Expanding the Canon." *Modern Philology* 89 (1991): 63.

Thelan, David. "Memory and American History." *Journal of American History* 75 (March 1989): 1117–1129.

Troncoso, Francisco P. *Las guerras con las tribus yaqui y mayo.* Mexico City: Instituto Nacional Indigenista, 1977.

Trujillo, Octaviana V. "The Yaqui of Guadalupe, Arizona: A Century of Cultural Survival through Trilingualism." *American Indian and Research Journal* 22, no. 4 (1998): 67–88.

Turner, Paul R. "Evaluating Religions: Religious and Behavioral Change in Missionary Conversations." *Missiology* (April 1991): 131–142.

Turner, Victor. *Forest of Symbols: Aspects of the Ndembu Ritual.* Ithaca, N.Y.: Cornell University, 1974.

Villa Rojas, Alfonso. "Notas sobre la etnografía de los indios tzeltales de Oxchuc, Chiapas, México." Microform. Chicago: University of Chicago Library, 1946.

Viqueira, Juan Pedro, and Mario Humberto Ruiz. *Chiapas: Los rumbos de otra historia.* Mexico City: Universidad Nacional Autónoma de México and Centro de Investigaciones y Estudios Superiores en Antropología Social (CIESAS), 1995.

Wagner-Pacifici, Robin, and Barry Schwartz. "The Vietnam Veterans Memorial: Commemorating a Difficult Past." *American Journal of Sociology* 97 (1991): 376–420.

Walsh, Michael J., trans. *Oscar Romero, Voice of the Voiceless: The Four Pastoral Letters and the Other Statements.* Maryknoll, N.Y.: Orbis Books, 1987.

Wasielewski, Henry. "Yaqui Lent and Easter Ceremonies 2000." 8 pp. Guadalupe, AZ: Our Lady of Guadalupe Church, 2000. Pamphlet.

Whiteman, Darrel. "Bible Translation and Social Cultural Development." In *Bible Translation and the Spread of the Church*, ed. Philip C. Stine, 120–144. Boston: Brill Academic Press, 1990.

Wild, Nette, dir. *A Place Called Chiapas.* New York: New York Film Studios, 2000.

Willard, William. "Self-government for Native Americans: The Case of the Pascua Yaqui Tribe." *Contributions in Political Science* 329 (1994): 1–13.

Wolf, Eric R. "The Virgin of Guadalupe: A Mexican National Symbol." *Journal of American Folklore* 71 (1958): 34–39.

Young, James E., ed. *The Art of Memory: Holocaust Memorials in History.* Munich: Prestel, 1994.
———. "A Holocaust Rorschach Test." *New York Times Magazine*, April 25, 1993, 36–39.
———. *The Texture of Memory: Holocaust Memorials and Meaning.* New Haven: Yale University Press, 1993.

Zatyrka, Alexander Paul. "The Formation of the Autochthonous Church and the Inculturation of the Christian Ministries in the Indian Cultures of America: A Case Study, the Bachajón Mission of the Diocese of San Cristóbal de las Casas, Mexico." Unpublished dissertation, Leopold Franzens Universität, Innsbruck, Austria, 2004.

Zelizer, Barbie. "Reading the Past against the Grain: The Shape of Memory Studies." *Critical Studies in Mass Communication* 12 (1995): 204–239.

Zerubavel, Eviatar. "Easter and Passover: On Calendars and Group Identity." *American Sociological Review* 47 (April 1982): 284–289.

Zerubavel, Yael. "The Death of Memory and the Memory of Death: Masada and the Holocaust as Historical Metaphors." *Representations* 45 (1994): 72–100.

———. "The Historic, the Legendary, and the Incredible: Invented Tradition and Collective Memory in Israel." In *Commemorations: The Politics of National Identity*, ed. John R. Gillis, 105–126. Princeton: Princeton University Press, 1994.

———. *Recovered Roots: Collective Memory and the Making of Israeli National Tradition*. Chicago: University of Chicago Press, 1995.

Zoontjens, Linda. "A Brief History of the Yaqui and Land." http://www.Sustained Action.org.explorations/history–of–the–yaqui.htm

Autobiographical Statements

Jeanette Rodríguez is a U.S. Hispanic/Latina theologian and Professor in the Department of Theology and Religious Studies at Seattle University. She received her Ph.D. at the Graduate Theological Union in Berkeley, California, and is author of *Our Lady of Guadalupe: Faith and Empowerment among Mexican American Women, Stories We Live*, and numerous articles on U.S. Hispanic theology, spirituality, and cultural memory. She also co-edited *A Reader in Latina Feminist Theology* with Maria Pilar Aquino and Daisy Machado.

Inspired by faith and the theologies of liberation, she directs her personal and professional commitments at the service of justice. This commitment takes the form of understanding, articulating, and offering the insights of the lived-faith experience of U.S. Latinos within the larger theological enterprise. In 2002, she was the recipient of the U.S. Catholic Award.

Ted Fortier, Associate Professor at Seattle University, cultural anthropologist, and former Jesuit priest, adds a significant dimension to this study. His research on the continuity of Indian Catholic identity on the Columbia Plateau and his book *Religion and Resistance in the Encounter between the Coeur d'Alene Indians and Jesuit Missionaries* both contribute to understanding the faith experience of Native Americans. His training as a cultural anthropologist, complemented by his background as a pastor and missionary among Native peoples, grounds his interest in cultural survival and allows him to access the manner in which cultural memory is key to the survival of cultural diversity.

Index

Jesuits *(continued)*: *reducciones,* 44,
128–129n.49; sixteenth-century
worldview of, 37–41; spirituality
of, 37–39; teaching tools used by,
129n.66; and Tzeltal Maya, 84–87, 96,
97, 102–103, 105, 131n.33; and Yaqui
Indians, 6, 37–44, 54
Jesuit University, El Salvador, 75–76
Jews, ix-x, xii, 4–5, 11–12
Jícaro cooperative, El Salvador, 66–67
JTijwanej method, 97–99
Juan Bernardino, 21, 22
Juan Carlos, 65–66, 68
Juan Diego, 17–24, 26, 31, 32, 48
Judeo-Christian tradition, 13. *See also*
Catholic Church

Kalpulli and *kallpulteol* (patron saint),
93, 94, 101
Kinship organization of Tzeltal Maya,
93, 94

Land reform in El Salvador, 57, 66
Las Casas, Fray Bartolomé de, 89, 97
Lasso de la Vega, Luis, 26
Latin American Bishop's Conference, 58
Let's Speak Clearly (radio program), 74
Liberation theology, 58–59, 75–76, 86,
130n.12
Lourdes, 25
Love: of God, 28, 31; and Our Lady of
Guadalupe, 29, 31–32, 34; Romero on
Christian love, 63. *See also* Theology
Lucius, Fr., 45
Lutes, Steven, 44
Lutheran University, 130n.12

Machismo, 66
Madre de los Pobres barrio, El Salvador,
71, 72–73
Marian shrines, 25
Marín, Luis, 89
Marriage of Tzeltal Maya, 93
Mary. *See* Our Lady of Guadalupe
Matachín Dancers, 48, 50, 51, 53
Maurer, Fr. Eugenio, 96, 100, 102, 103,
131n.31

Maya, 16, 42, 68, 88. *See also* Tzeltal
Maya
Mazariegos, Diego de, 89
McGuire, Thomas R., 35, 37, 49
Meals. *See* Food
Memorial War, El Salvador, 76–77
Memory. *See* Christian memory;
Cultural memory; Historical memory
Méndez, Fr. Pedro, 128n.42
Metz, Johann Baptist, 5, 23, 28
Mexican Americans: and Our Lady
of Guadalupe, 4, 5, 15–16, 27–34;
struggle by, for finding a place, 1–2
Mexico: expulsion of Catholic Church
from, and Mexican Revolution, 86,
89–90, 95; independence of, 97;
indigenous movements in, 113–117,
119–120; presidents of, 113–117;
religious history of, 16–17; San
Andrés Accords in, 95, 117, 121–124;
Spanish Conquest of, 16, 17, 25, 27,
41, 89, 130–131n.12; summary of post-
independence political movements
in, 113–117; Yaqui in, 41–45, 54.
See also Chiapas, Mexico; Tzeltal
Maya
Meyers, Rev. Dave, 46, 50
Miller, Judith, 11
Missionaries. *See* Franciscans; Jesuits
Montesquieu, Baron de, 44
Montezuma I, 16
Montezuma II, 16
Monumentos Guadalupanos, 26
Morales, Nacho, 103
Moreno, Gilberto, 102, 103
Mothers of the Disappeared (Co-
Madres), 70–71, 76, 82, 109–110
Music: and Our Lady of Guadalupe, 18,
31; and Romero memory, 73–74, 79,
80, 81, 83; and Yaqui ceremonies, 35,
43, 47, 51
Mythopoesis, 48
Myths: cultural memory compared
with, 12–13; definition of, 12, 125n.16;
Nahuatl mythology, 16–17, 19–20, 25;
origin myths, 129n.68; of Our Lady of
Guadalupe, 12, 17–25, 48–49